WHAT EVERY MANAGER SHOULD KNOW ABOUT FINANCIAL ANALYSIS

Alan S. Donnahoe

Simon and Schuster

New York London Toronto Sydney Tokyo

SIMON AND SCHUSTER
Simon & Schuster Building
Rockefeller Center
1230 Avenue of the Americas
New York, New York 10020

Designed by Irving Perkins Associates
Manufactured in the United States of America

1 3 5 7 9 10 8 6 4 2

Library of Congress Cataloging-in-Publication Data

Donnahoe, Alan S.
What every manager should know about financial analysis / Alan S. Donnahoe.
p. cm.
Includes index.
1. Corporations—Finance. I. Title.
HG4026.D645 1989 *89-6313*
658.15—dc20 *CIP*

ISBN 0-671-61098-8

ACKNOWLEDGMENTS

My gratitude to my colleagues over the years for teaching me many lessons about the business world, and for their guidance and cooperation in coping with all the challenges inherent in the management of a fast-growing company.

My sincere appreciation as well to Frederic W. Hills, vice-president and senior editor of Simon and Schuster, for his unfailing encouragement and support from the beginning of this book to its completion.

In addition, for their valuable assistance in the preparation of this book, special thanks are due to Samuel A. Derieux, a partner of Deloitte Haskins & Sells and a former president and chairman of the board of the American Institute of Certified Public Accountants, and to my son-in-law, C. Porter Vaughan III, a partner of Hunton & Williams who specializes in securities law. Although they have been most helpful with their technical knowledge of the subject, any errors in this book are mine alone.

To
E.P.D.
and
K.D.V.

CONTENTS

PREFACE

Do you feel lost in dealing with financial data of any kind, as if you were drowning in a sea of strange numbers? Are you frightened by a financial statement and panic-stricken at the thought of interpreting a balance sheet or preparing a departmental budget?

If this description fits you, take comfort in the knowledge that you are far from alone. There are hundreds of thousands of other executives and managers for whom the same is true. And they no doubt feel equally lost, because the inability to understand and deal with financial data is a severe handicap in the corporate world.

In a very real sense, finance is the language of business. Goals are set and performance is measured in financial terms. Plants are built, equipment ordered, and new projects undertaken based on clear investment return criteria. Financial analysis is required in every such case.

If you are truly concerned about your lack of understanding of this subject, then this book is for you. It is written for the executive or manager with a minimum of time to spend. It does not require that you go back to school, or learn a lot of complicated accounting principles, or cope with difficult mathematical formulas. You will find this book easy to read because it is written in very simple language without all the jargon that sometimes surrounds and obscures the subject. Many examples are used to illustrate and clarify the key points involved, with charts and tables added when they can be helpful.

Throughout the book, every effort is made to present the subject of financial analysis in its true perspective, including its significance and usefulness to top management. This perspective can be very useful in the career growth of any manager. The book also covers some topics, such as the financial framework of compensation systems, not normally found in books on this subject; but these are important for anyone who wants to understand the language of finance in its fullest sense.

Finally, you will quickly see that this book is based on my long experience as a chief executive officer, with many practical insights that should be helpful to a manager at any level in dealing with real problems in a corporate environment. And because it is also based on principles that endure, you will find it a handy reference that you can return to from time to time whenever you need to refresh your memory.

Thus, there is no longer any need for you to feel lost in the world of finance. You will find that mastering the techniques of financial analysis is both a practical and an exciting experience.

CHAPTER 1

OVERHEAD: A CAUTIONARY TALE

ANYONE WHO STARTS a small business, or who has to meet a weekly payroll, is keenly aware of the need to earn a profit, for enough revenue to cover expenses with something to spare. Intelligent expense control is essential in any well-managed company. In small companies, expenses can usually be measured clearly and simply. In large corporations, by contrast, expenses may vary greatly from division to division, and it is important for you as a manager to understand just how they are defined and allocated.

Expenses fall into two major categories: fixed and variable. Fixed expenses are those that remain the same, irrespective of production or sales volume. They are called overhead, and represent a special concern to management. These are the expenses that must be covered, in good times and bad, and they determine the breakeven point of the company. Thus all good managers are expected to work hard to control, and if possible to reduce, all the elements that enter into overhead expense.

Special problems arise in large companies in the treatment of overhead expense in their internal accounting statements, and how this is handled can affect every manager in the company. It is a great mistake to leave this matter to accounting personnel without a clear understanding by top executives of the methods being used and their impact on policy decisions.

DANGERS IN OVERHEAD ALLOCATION

In many and perhaps most corporations, directors are shown profit by division or subsidiary after allocation of corporate overhead, a practice that has never appealed to me. Here is one reason I feel that way.

The directors of Company X were given the following profit report for the year:

(IN $MILLIONS)

DIVISION	PROFIT	OVERHEAD	REMAINDER
A	10	12	−2
B	20	15	5
C	30	20	10
Total	60	47	13

The directors noted that Division A was operating at a loss and decided to sell it. Corporate overhead assigned to that division was then reallocated to the other two, and the annual report was revised as follows:

(IN $MILLIONS)

DIVISION	PROFIT	OVERHEAD	REMAINDER
B	20	21	−1
C	30	26	4
Total	50	47	3

The directors now saw that Division B was losing money, and decided to sell that as well. All the corporate overhead now fell on the remaining division, and the revised annual report looked like this:

(IN $MILLIONS)			
DIVISION	PROFIT	OVERHEAD	REMAINDER
C	30	47	−13
Total	30	47	−13

With the enterprise now deeply in the red, the directors sadly concluded they had no alternative but to liquidate the company.

All this nonsense would have been avoided, of course, if the first report to the directors had read as follows:

PROFIT CONTRIBUTION	
DIVISION	$MILLIONS
A	10
B	20
C	30
Total	60
Overhead	47
Profit	13

While this example is exaggerated, it clearly illustrates that it can be very dangerous to make any business decision based on profit totals, by division or subsidiary, that have been adjusted to absorb corporate overhead.

OTHER PROBLEMS IN ALLOCATION

There are other reasons why I have no enthusiasm for this procedure. First of all, any allocation of overhead expense must be arbitrary because, by definition, overhead is something that is not traceable or related to any specific unit of the company. There is no sensible way, for example, to allocate the salary of the president, or rent of corporate headquarters, among a number of operating units.

If overhead is prorated according to the sales of each operating unit, the net effect is to penalize the unit with a below-average profit margin. If the proration is based on the total profit of each unit, then clearly the higher the profit the greater the penalty. And so it goes, from one distortion to another. Where this procedure is followed, I think there is a reasonable doubt that even the chief financial officer fully understands all the implications of overhead allocation, and it is a fair bet that the CEO is even more fuzzy about it.

All this can create serious morale problems at the division or subsidiary level when these managers see their profits sharply reduced by some charge for corporate overhead about which they know nothing, and for which they have no responsibility whatsoever. And their resentment can become quite intense if these adjusted profit figures have anything to do with executive bonus calculations!

There is always a natural tendency for division and subsidiary executives to have a small private war going with corporate headquarters: a little *them* versus *us* psychology. Obviously there is no merit in this attitude in terms of overall company morale, and thus I always find it surprising that companies would add to the problem with this overhead allocation procedure.

RATIONALE FOR THE ALLOCATION PROCEDURE

Why, then, do so many companies follow this procedure? The only answer I can give is that it seems to be the traditional practice, and many executives have been trained to expect it and simply consider it the proper thing to do. I have known some very talented CEOs, for example, who view it as a harsh discipline that simply must be imposed: "This overhead exists, and must be charged to the operating units so neither they nor we will be under any illusion as to our true profit status!"

All this, in my view, is pure nonsense. I think the only proper way to treat overhead expense is to itemize it and put it on a separate page like any other profit (loss) center. Overhead is the specific responsibility of the chief executive officer, and it should be separately itemized and reported as such.

But merely to cite this alternative is enough to make it crystal clear why many CEOs are fond of the traditional overhead-allocation system. It is a clever vanishing act that makes overhead disappear on reports to the board of directors, so that no one, including the CEO, needs to take any responsibility for it. An ingenious bit of magic and a very comfortable procedure indeed!

WHAT CAN YOU DO?

If an overhead allocation system is followed in your company, there is not much likelihood that you can do very much to change it, for all the reasons given above. Arguing about any specific allocation is likely to be a waste of time. The accountants have doubtless worked up an elaborate scheme to accomplish this, and any attempt to alter the procedure is certain to run into strong resistance.

But what you should insist on, for your department or division, is that accounting reports clearly specify profit before and after overhead allocation. This is sound procedure and accountants should agree with it accordingly. But if there is any problem here, and the reporting format does not make the distinction entirely clear, then a supplement should be prepared to highlight these two figures.

Now, you and your associates should concentrate on profit before overhead allocation. This is something you can do something about, and it is the true measure of how well your group is performing. It is also the figure that should be used internally for performance bonuses and the like, and the figure that should be emphasized in reports to senior officers of the company.

In brief, your best procedure is to treat the overhead allocation as the fiction that it is and fix your attention on the reality of profit contribution before such allocation. You may reasonably assume that most senior executives who review the performance of your group understand reality, and will be in full accord with this approach.

SUMMARY

Allocation of corporate overhead among divisions and departments is standard procedure in most large companies, and this procedure is not likely to change, for a variety of reasons. But there are real dangers in this procedure, which can seriously distort the performance of the various operating units within the company. This, in turn, can lead to some very bad management decisions.

As a manager in such a corporation, the main thing you can do is to be certain that accounting reports for your group show profit before and after overhead allocation. You cannot do much if anything about the allocation, which is essentially arbitrary and fictitious, but you can concentrate on and do something about profit contribution before allocation, which is the real measure of performance.

CHAPTER 2

HOW TO READ A FINANCIAL STATEMENT

THE FINANCIAL PROFILE of a company is outlined in its profit and loss statement and balance sheet, and every manager should know how to read and interpret that profile.

While public companies publish interim statements quarterly, these usually are quite brief, and for full details one must turn to the company's published annual report. For purposes of illustration, I have selected such a report more or less at random from a company that manufactures and distributes printed forms, computer supplies, and the like. The name of the company, for which reporting dates have been changed, is not material to our purposes here, and thus it will be called Company X.

Starting with the *Consolidated Balance Sheet* (Table 2.1), we see several items grouped under the heading *Current Assets.* Typically, these are items that can be converted into cash within a year. The first such item in the Company X statement for Year 2 is $30,817,000 in *Cash and short-term investments.* This is a large sum for a company of this size, especially in relation to its debt and other liabilities, as we shall see later.

We cannot tell from this entry how much of this sum is in actual cash, as distinguished from short-term investments, but most companies work hard these days on cash

Table 2.1

CONSOLIDATED BALANCE SHEET

(In Thousands of Dollars)

	Year 2	Year 1
Assets		
Current Assets		
Cash and short-term investments	$ 30,817	$ 31,784
Accounts receivable, less allowance for doubtful accounts of $1,544 in 1986 and $1,521 in 1985	49,219	41,646
Inventories	41,628	34,462
Advances and prepaid expenses	5,772	4,638
Total current assets	**127,436**	**112,530**
Property, Plant, and Equipment, at Cost		
Land and buildings	45,523	32,747
Machinery, equipment, furniture, and fixtures	106,127	94,140
Leasehold improvements	1,025	929
Total property, plant, and equipment	152,675	127,816
Less—reserves for depreciation and amortization	56,144	49,823
Net property, plant, and equipment	**96,531**	**77,993**
Funds Held by Trustee for Construction	—	**3,484**
Intangible Assets Arising from Acquisition	**1,382**	**1,382**
Total assets	**$225,349**	**$195,389**
Liabilities and Stockholders' Equity		
Current Liabilities		
Current maturities of long-term debt	$ 320	$ 295
Accounts payable	12,893	12,733
Dividends payable	1,275	1,135
Accrued salaries, wages, and taxes	13,160	12,631
Contribution to profit-sharing and retirement fund	4,867	4,410
Federal and state income taxes	4,061	806
Total current liabilities	**36,576**	**32,010**

Table 2.1 (Continued)

CONSOLIDATED BALANCE SHEET

(In Thousands of Dollars)

	Year 2	Year 1
Deferred Income Taxes	**16,050**	**12,540**
Long-term Debt	**14,520**	**14,840**
Stockholders' Equity		
Preferred stock, $50 par value, authorized 500,000 shares	—	—
Common stock, $1.00 par value, authorized 30,000,000 shares	10,200	10,087
Additional capital	15,057	12,240
Retained earnings	132,946	113,672
Total stockholders' equity	**158,203**	**135,999**
Total liabilities	**$225,349**	**$195,389**

management, which means keeping actual cash to an absolute minimum and investing the remainder in short-term earning assets. About the only major exception to this is when a company is required to keep some compensating balance with a bank as a condition for a bank loan or line of credit. This is a matter of negotiation, and sometimes the company prefers to pay a service fee of some kind in lieu of the compensating balance.

The next item in the balance sheet is $49,219,000 in *Accounts receivable, less allowance for doubtful accounts.* After cash and equivalents, this is the next most liquid asset on the balance sheet, normally convertible to cash in a relatively short period. Indeed, when accounts receivable are added to cash and short-term investments, we have what analysts call quick assets. For Company X, the quick assets total some $80 million, which, once again, is a very large sum for a company of this size.

We can test the liquidity and relative age of accounts receivable by dividing total sales (see Table 2.2) by 365 to get average sales per day (which works out to be about

$836,000 in this case), and dividing this into the total of accounts receivable to find the average number of days' sales that accounts receivable represents. For Company X, this turns out to be an average of 58.9 days.

This is a somewhat longer age period than you may find with many companies, but the period can vary from one line of business to another, depending on trade practices, and this can be checked by looking at similar ratios for other companies in the same industry. Seasonal sales trends can affect this ratio and that should be considered as well. It may also be useful to see what change has occurred in the ratio in the given company over time. In the year before, for example, the average was 55.4 days of sales in accounts receivable, so there has been a slight increase of the age of accounts, but nothing material in the way of change.

Next on the balance sheet is $41,628,000 for *Inventories.* In the specified footnote to the balance sheet this figure is broken down to about $17 million in raw materials, $2 million of work in progress, and $23 million in finished products.

If you look at a balance sheet in terms of actual values that might be realized if the company were liquidated, any discount from stated values would doubtless increase as you go backward in this chain from finished products to raw materials, so the breakdown in the footnote is significant.

To check the inventory total in terms of reasonableness, it is useful to divide it into total sales to get a measure of turnover. For Company X, this turnover ratio is 7.3 ($305,044 divided by $41,628). In other words, the inventory represents about one and one-half months of sales. Once again, this ratio can be expected to vary rather sharply by line of business, but it certainly looks quite reasonable for this particular company.

To be entirely precise, the turnover ratio should be divided into total cost of sales, instead of total sales, and it is exaggerated somewhat by using the latter. But this further detail is often not available, and no great error is involved if this refinement is ignored in comparing one company with another.

The balance sheet note says that inventory is valued at cost, not to exceed market, and that some components were valued by the LIFO method and others by the FIFO method. It is important to understand the distinction between LIFO and FIFO. *LIFO* means last-in, first-out. A typical illustration is inventory in the form of a coal pile. As new coal is purchased, it is put on top of the pile. As coal is withdrawn from the inventory, it is taken from the top. Thus the cost of the entire inventory is based on the most recent purchase price.

FIFO means first-in, first-out. In the coal analogy, coal is withdrawn from the bottom of the pile, and cost of the inventory is based on historical costs. The net effect of this is that in times of inflation and rising costs, the FIFO method tends to understate the true cost of the inventory and overstate profits accordingly.

To avoid this, many companies have gone to the LIFO system. The benefit has been a saving in income taxes and more conservative accounting in times of inflation, even though it involves a reduction in reported net income. It should be recognized, of course, that LIFO may understate the amount of inventory reported on the balance sheet.

Companies differ in their operating structure, and LIFO is not always appropriate, but financial analysts pay close attention to how the cost of inventory is calculated in each case, for all the reasons given above.

The last item in current assets is $5,772,000 in *Advances and prepaid expenses.* In the normal course of business, companies will pay certain expenses in advance, such as insurance premiums. This total, once again, seems quite reasonable.

When all these items are added, the result is a total of $127,436,000 for all current assets. By itself, of course, this figure means very little, but it becomes highly significant when compared with liabilities shown on the same balance sheet, as we shall see a little later.

TANGIBLE AND OTHER ASSETS

Continuing with the *Assets* section of the balance sheet, we next see a value of $45,523,000 for *Land and buildings,* a value of $106,127,000 for *Machinery, equipment, furniture, and fixtures,* and a value of $1,025,000 for *Leasehold improvements,* with the last representing sums spent in improving rental quarters.

Because buildings, machinery, and equipment deteriorate over time and must one day be replaced, a depreciation reserve is set up to anticipate this cost. For Company X, this reserve amounts to $56,144,000, and when this is subtracted from the gross values of the various assets, the net value of *Property, plant, and equipment* becomes $96,531,000. As distinguished from cash or liquid assets, these are the tangible assets of the company and their net book value.

I say book value because these assets are carried on the books of the company at the total indicated, but you should be aware that this value can differ considerably from the real or market value of the assets. Typically, they are carried on the books at their historical cost, less depreciation, and this may be a considerable distortion of real value on a current basis.

Very often, because of rising costs over the years, the depreciation allowance on the books is wholly inadequate to meet the true cost of replacement when that need occurs. On the other hand, land values have grown rapidly in many areas of the country, and certain land and building values carried on the books of some companies are only a fraction of what the assets could be sold for.

In brief, the tangible asset values reported in a balance sheet are interesting, but you should be aware that they may differ materially from true or fair market value. To get some proper estimate of this requires, typically, a detailed analysis by trained appraisers.

Returning to the balance sheet, the final asset listed is a total of $1,382,000 for *Intangible Assets Arising From Acquisition.* This is a rather formal phrase for what is generally called goodwill, which comes about when a company acquires another company for more than the latter's net worth. The difference between the purchase price and net worth of the company acquired is goodwill, which is carried on the books as an intangible value, typically being amortized and written off year by year over a period of time.

Companies don't like to put goodwill on their balance sheets, but they are required to do so by accounting rules. They don't like it because it usually must be charged off over a period of years, thus reducing reported net income without any offsetting tax benefit—a very disagreeable combination!

The total is almost negligible in the Company X balance sheet, but in general it is very difficult for an outsider to evaluate what intangible values really mean. Sometimes the company that was acquired is worth far more than the original purchase price, and in that case the goodwill total would materially understate the true value involved. And, of course, the opposite can be true as well.

In loan agreements of various kinds, with restrictive covenants based on net worth, it is a common requirement that all intangible values be eliminated so that net worth, in effect, becomes tangible net worth. This is a rather clear indication that lenders, in general, prefer to put their faith in tangible values only. But it is also true that they sometimes recognize clear exceptions to the rule. Perhaps the best insight into all this was provided many years ago by a distinguished analyst who said that the only real test of intangible values must be found in the profit and loss statement, in terms of income being generated, and it is difficult to argue with that position.

Finally we come to *Total assets,* the grand total of all the assets listed, $225,349,000. In comparing various companies, this is one of the standard measures of size (the other being total sales), and the $225 million total tells us that this is a medium-size company. These standards are not absolute, but at this time $100 million in assets is perhaps a reasonable breakpoint between small and medium-size companies, and $500 million in assets a similar dividing line between medium-size and large companies.

LIABILITIES

Now that we have seen the asset side of the balance sheet, let's turn to the liability side: what the company owes to others. Six items are listed under *Current Liabilities.* These represent sums that will be due and must be paid within one year, the same period involved in classifying current assets.

Most of these items are self-explanatory: $320,000 in *Current maturities of long-term debt;* $12,893,000 in *Accounts payable,* which the company owes its various suppliers and others; $1,275,000 in *Dividends payable,* which the company has declared but not yet paid; and $13,160,000 in *Accrued salaries, wages, and taxes,* which includes time worked but not yet paid for, accrued vacations, payroll taxes, and the like. Then there is $4,867,000 for *Contribution to profit-sharing and retirement fund,* and finally, $4,061,000 in *Federal and state income taxes* that have accrued.

All these items total $36,576,000, and we must gauge the significance of this by comparison with other totals in the balance sheet. The obvious counterpart to current liabilities is current assets: what the company owes within a year versus what it can convert into cash in the same period. And in this case we have current liabilities of less than $37 million versus current assets of more than $127 million. The difference between these two, about $90 million in this case, is called *working capital,* which is the amount available to meet current operating needs of the company. This is a relatively huge amount, for a company of this size, and there can be no question about its adequacy.

Current assets divided by current liabilities is called the *current ratio,* and as the total of working capital would suggest, the Company X ratio of 3.5 is very high indeed. Although it will vary by line of business, a current ratio of 2.0 is considered to be quite strong, and the median for public companies today is 1.7.

There are some exceptions to this measure of strength in capital intensive companies, such as trucking companies, that may be financially sound even though their current ratio is negative. The reason, of course, is that they produce their revenue from fixed assets instead of the sale of inventory items.

Still another insight is provided by what is called the *quick ratio,* in which the total of cash and accounts receivable (the *quick assets*) is compared with current liabilities. These quick assets for Company X amount to $80,036,000, which is 2.2 times the total for current liabilities. Here again, with a quick ratio of 1.0 normally considered quite satisfactory, the 2.2 ratio indicates unusual financial strength.

So we can conclude that Company X is viewed as a first-class credit risk by its suppliers and others who extend it credit in the normal course of business. On the other hand, if a company is substandard in either of these key ratios, there will be appropriate caution on the part of its trade and other creditors.

The next item on the balance sheet is $16,050,000 in *Deferred income taxes* and the footnote explains this is mainly due to accelerated depreciation for income tax purposes and to the amortizing of investment tax credits over the life of the asset. In the past, companies have typically kept two sets of books—one for tax purposes and another for reporting income—and entries of this type are needed to reconcile the two.

There is nothing sinister about this practice. Tax laws change constantly, and tax credits can materially distort reported net income in any given year. So companies naturally take the tax credits when available, but try to avoid the distortion this might otherwise create in reported earnings.

DEBT AND NET WORTH

Returning to our balance sheet, we next see $14,520,000 in *Long-term Debt,* which means debt coming due after twelve months. This is a key item on any balance sheet but, again, it must be analyzed in terms of other elements of the balance sheet, including the one that follows designated as *Stockholders' Equity.* This category reflects what the owners of the business have put into it, either through purchase of its stock or in the form of earnings that have been retained and not paid out in dividends. What they have put into the company by buying its stock is shown in the $10,200,000 and $15,057,000 totals for *Common stock* and *Additional capital,* and this plus the $132,946,000 in *Retained earnings* makes up the grand total of $158,203,000 in stockholders' equity.

Preferred stock has been authorized by stockholders of the company, but none has been issued. Preferred stock, as the name indicates, takes precedence over common stock in the payment of dividends and in liquidation of the company. To the common stockholder, therefore, preferred stock is a liability comparable to bonds or other debt. In terms of corporate financing, the disadvantage is that dividends on preferred stock, unlike interest on debt, is not tax deductible. But companies are sometimes forced to use it, nevertheless, for various reasons including loan agreement covenants that prohibit adding any further debt.

Coming back to stockholders' equity, you may be puzzled to find that it is included under liabilities. But this, in essence, is what the company owes its stockholders; and when it is included as part of liabilities, total liabilities must be equal to total assets. Put another way, when you subtract all other liabilities from total assets, stockholders' equity is what is left over: the difference between the two.

Thus stockholders' equity is often called the net worth of a company, what it would be worth in liquidation, assuming that all values stated on the balance sheet are precisely correct. For the same reason, it is often referred to as the book value of the company.

For all the reasons that have been mentioned, the true or market values of assets may differ materially from those listed on the balance sheet and the true net worth of the company will vary accordingly. This, in turn, may differ materially from the going value of the company in terms of income-producing power. With Company X, for example, this is underlined by a stock price high of $50.00 per share in the fourth quarter of the year, compared with a book value of only $15.79 per share.

Even with all these qualifications, however, book value is a significant figure, especially in its relationship to other items on the balance sheet. Long-term debt is an illustration. It is logical to compare the total of such debt to the net worth or book value of the company. For Company X, this debt is only 9 percent of net worth, which is a relatively low figure compared with the current median among public companies of 31 percent.

Again, there are no absolute benchmarks for how much debt a company should have, but in general this debt ratio is an index to the relative conservatism of management, whether past or present. And there are a fair number of companies with no debt at all, which is the ultimate in financial conservatism.

In general, however, if the debt to equity ratio is no more than 50 percent, it would be considered reasonable by most analysts. Beyond that, the company begins to move into the "high-leverage" category, meaning that debt is being used to a significant degree to lever the total capitalization of the company. And when the ratio of debt to equity reaches 100 percent, then the company is very definitely in the high-leverage group.

As in many things in life, there is a risk/reward relationship here. Clearly, the more debt a company has in relation to its net worth, the riskier it becomes, just as would be the case with an individual. On the other hand, if debt is a relatively cheap source of capital, and a company can use the capital to produce a strong income return, then clearly it will profit by the use of such debt.

Still another consideration in the dog-eat-dog corporate world of today is that a company with little or no debt is a very tempting takeover target, because the company's unused debt capacity can be used against it, in effect, to finance purchase of its stock, with a minimum burden on the raider. Consequently, as a matter of self-defense, many companies of this type have installed various legal obstacles to inhibit or thwart an unfriendly takeover.

In any event, coming back to Company X, we have seen that it has an exceptionally strong current ratio and quick ratio, and now we see that it has a low ratio of debt to equity. All this adds up to a company of unusual financial strength, and without knowing any more than these three ratios, we can deduce that it has been operated by very conservative management.

Now, the question is what this management has been able to accomplish on the income side. Clearly it is financially strong, but is it also effective in terms of profitability? To answer this, we need to turn to the *Consolidated Statement of Income* (Table 2.2).

The first line in Table 2.2 shows that *Net Sales* for the last fiscal year were $305,044,000. This is the gross income of the company, from which all expenses must be paid, with the remainder as the profit for the year.

Under *Costs and Expenses,* the largest item is the $190,930,000 in *Costs of goods sold.* Next is $61,830,000 in *Selling and administrative expenses.* Following this is

Table 2.2

CONSOLIDATED STATEMENT OF INCOME
(In Thousands Except per Share Amounts)

	Year 2	Year 1	Year 0
Net Sales	$305,044	$274,595	$243,125
Costs and Expenses			
Cost of goods sold	190,930	172,163	157,319
Selling and administrative expenses	61,830	55,415	45,657
Provision for depreciation and amortization	8,730	7,155	6,262
Interest income, net	(1,539)	(1,740)	(1,301)
Total costs and expenses	259,951	232,993	207,937
Income Before Income Taxes	45,093	41,602	35,188
Provision for Income Taxes			
Current			
Federal	14,168	13,616	12,216
State	3,065	2,894	2,208
Deferred	3,510	3,043	2,115
Total income taxes	20,743	19,553	16,539
Net Income	$ 24,350	$ 22,049	$ 18,649
Net Income per Share	$2.40	$2.20	$1.90

$8,730,000 in *Provision for depreciation and amortization,* which is not a cash but rather a bookkeeping reserve set aside for replacement of machinery and equipment. The last item of $1,539,000 is for *Interest income, net,* and is in parentheses. This means that this much interest was earned on investments in excess of interest paid, so the listed amount is an offset to other expenses.

Total costs and expenses add to $259,951,000 and when this is subtracted from net sales, we get $45,093,000 as the *Income Before Income Taxes.* From this figure must be deducted $20,743,000 in federal and state income taxes, current and deferred, to get the *Net Income*—or profit—of $24,350,000, which is equal to $2.40 per share.

Remember that $8,730,000 in depreciation allowance was deducted in arriving at this total, and because it is a book reserve only and not a cash expenditure, it must be added back to net income to get the cash flow of the company. This amounts to $33,080,000 and represents cash available to pay for capital outlays, make principal payments on debt, and pay dividends.

It is important to look at cash flow because it is perhaps the key index of a company's ability to meet its basic needs. Net income alone can sometimes be misleading in this respect, and especially so, of course, when depreciation allowances are relatively large.

Again, to fully understand the significance of these totals, they must be placed in context in relation to other items in the income statement and balance sheet. For example, net income as a percentage of net sales is the *profit margin* of a company, and this ratio for Company X is 8.0 percent. The ratio will tend to vary by line of business, but the profit margin for this company is certainly much higher than the 4.9 percent current median for all public companies.

If a company has a higher profit margin than others in the same line of business, this suggests a greater degree of management efficiency, and of course the contrary is true as well. But beyond this, a good profit margin is an insurance policy against future changes of an adverse nature in the business environment. This is clear enough when you think about a very low profit margin, where a few percentage points are the difference between operating at a loss and operating at a profit. So, once again, Company X passes this test with flying colors.

RETURN ON EQUITY

But important as the profit margin is, it only tells part of the story. A company can have a high profit margin and still earn a very poor profit total in relation to its size and the capital invested in it. To check this we need to look at net income as a percentage of stockholders' equity: what the company is earning, in effect, on the capital entrusted to it by its owners.

For Company X, the return on stockholders' equity is 15.4 percent. This is a good ratio, and compares with a current median of 12.6 percent for all profitable public companies. But Company X's performance is really better than this comparison indicates when we consider its capital structure and relatively small debt component.

In other words, a company can leverage its return on equity by adding debt to its balance sheet, and there is very little such leveraging on the part of Company X. To eliminate the leveraging factor, we can look at net income as a percentage of total assets. In this return on assets, the Company X ratio of 10.8 percent is more than four times the current median of 2.6 percent for all public companies.

Once again, therefore, we see the profile of a very conservative company, financially strong with very little debt, that still manages to make a very good return on its invested equity. All this speaks exceedingly well for the company and for its management.

One thing further remains, and that is the question of growth. Sometimes very strong and conservative companies have exhausted their growth potential, and can look forward only to stagnation or gradual deterioration. Although the past is no certain guide to the future, a quick check on this is the earnings trend over a period of years. For Company X, this trend has been consistently up, year after year, over a period of many years. Unless there is some specific indication to the contrary, this is strong evidence that the earnings of Company X will continue to grow.

SUMMARY

I selected Company X at random for purposes of this chapter and, beyond this, know nothing about the company at all. My analysis, therefore, is based entirely on its financial statements, and it is easy enough for you to follow the same procedure and make the same analysis from the same material.

The point, of course, is that you can acquire a remarkable amount of information, and tell a great deal about a company, from its financial statements alone, and thus it is highly useful for any manager to understand this material. The time you spend learning to read a balance sheet and income statement will be very well spent indeed.

CHAPTER 3

THE POWER OF COMPOUND INTEREST

As we all know, money is not a free commodity, and a rental fee, in the form of interest, is normally charged for its use. It is very helpful for anyone, and especially so for managers, to understand how this rental fee is computed. The arithmetic involved is very easy, but nevertheless, many people are not altogether clear about it. This can be a real handicap for managers who must sometimes come up with a quick answer to questions about the cost of money. So let's see how all this works.

There are two types of interest: simple and compound. *Simple interest* on a principal amount (and only on the principal) invested or borrowed remains fixed at a given rate throughout the length of the investment or loan. Thus, with $1,000 invested at 10 percent interest per year, the annual interest will be $100 throughout the term of investment.

With *compound interest,* by contrast, interest each year is added to the principal amount in computing interest for the following year. With $1,000 invested or borrowed at 10 percent compound interest, therefore, the interest will be $100 the first year, $110 the second year, $121 the third year, and so on.

As time goes on, this payment of interest on accumulated interest can make a big difference. Over a period of ten years, for example, $1,000 invested at 10 percent grows to $2,000 at simple interest and to $2,594 at compound interest, which makes it quite clear why neither investors nor lenders find much appeal in simple interest.

It is inherent in the law of compound interest that although the rate remains constant, the actual amount being accumulated will accelerate as the years go on, with some rather astonishing results. For example: $1.00 invested at 10 percent per year for 100 years will grow to $13,781. This is not bad, but there is much more to come. After 200 years that original dollar will have grown to $189,905,276, and after 300 years to more than $2.6 trillion. And for still longer periods, the total explodes to even greater astronomical size, far exceeding the money supply of the world.

Now, let's take a look at the simple arithmetic that is involved in all this magic by continuing with our example of $1.00 invested at 10 percent per year. After one year you will have $1.00 plus 10 cents interest for a total of $1.10. In the second year, interest is 10 percent of $1.10, or 11 cents, and your investment has grown to $1.21. In the third year, interest is 10 percent of $1.21, or 12.1 cents, and your investment has grown to $1.331. And so on.

Now, note that if your interest rate is expressed as a ratio instead of a percentage (.10 = 10 percent), you can add this to your original $1.00 (giving you 1.10), and by multiplying this number by itself come up with the same answers shown above. Thus, for one year, you have 1.10 × 1, which is $1.10. For two years you have 1.10 × 1.10, which is equal to $1.21. And for three years you have 1.10 × 1.10 × 1.10, which is equal to $1.331. And so on.

It is just as simple as that. To find the cumulative value of $1.00 invested at compound interest, simply add the interest rate in ratio form to 1, and then multiply that number by itself as many times as the number of years in which the compounding takes place.

For those who like equations, this can be expressed as follows with *Rate* being the interest rate in ratio form, *N* being the number of years involved, and *Value* being the cumulative value of $1 invested at the compound rate of interest:

$$\text{Value} = (1 + \text{Rate})^{N}$$

Now, you may say, all this is fine but I am investing (or borrowing) much more than a single dollar, so how does all this help me? Again, the answer is very simple. You first get the answer for one dollar, as shown above, and then multiply this by the total dollars involved in the initial investment or loan.

You have just seen, for example, that $1.00 at 10 percent interest will grow to $1.331 in three years. If you invested $1,000 dollars at this rate, therefore, it would grow to $1,331 in three years (1,000 × 1.331). It is no more complicated than that. In fact, you don't even have to do the arithmetic yourself when simple, inexpensive calculators can do the job in a few seconds.

CALCULATING PROCEDURE

All you need is a calculator with a power key (usually designated by "y^x") that will calculate what a number is to any given power, which is the same as multiplying the number by itself that many times.

Thus, to find the cumulative value of $1.00 at the end of three years with compound interest at 10 percent per year, you simply enter 1.10 in the machine, press the "y^x" key and then enter 3 followed by the "=" key, and the 1.331 answer will appear. This is the way you take 1.10 to the third power. Using exactly the same procedure, you can check the amounts listed earlier in this chapter for cumulated values after 100, 200, and 300 years.

It is remarkable how quickly a calculator can do all this work: the result of hundreds of multiplications is arrived at with nothing more than the entry of two numbers along with pressing the power key and the equal key. But be certain that you get a calculator with a power key, and also note that some calculators require that the two numbers be entered in reverse sequence from that described above.

HOW TO FIND THE INTEREST RATE

Now, you have seen how easy it is to measure the cumulative value of $1.00 at any given rate of compound interest. The next question is: Can you reverse the process? In other words, if you know the cumulative value that $1.00 has grown to over a given number of years, how can you find the rate of interest involved?

Again, the calculator will give you this answer very quickly. Let's assume that your cumulative value at the end of three years is $1.331. You enter 1.331 in the calculator, press the "y^x" key, and then enter 1/3 (.3333) and press the "=" key and 1.10 appears as the answer. Subtract 1 and the remainder of .10, or 10 percent, is the answer.

What you have done here is take the third root of your 1.331 cumulative value, which gives you the number that, when multiplied by itself three times, equals that cumulative value. And this number, of course, is "1 + Rate," so you must deduct 1 to get the interest rate in ratio form.

To work this out it may be easier to first enter the number of years, 3 in this case, and touch the reciprocal key (1/x) to get the value of 1/3; then press the memory key to hold this value. Then, when it comes time to enter the value of 1/3, you simply recall the value from the calculator memory.

I recommend that you spend a few minutes with your calculator to work out some examples of this kind, until the process becomes quite familiar. You will find it will become very simple and easy. You will also find it extremely useful in various aspects of financial analysis.

GROWTH RATES

The process of finding the rate of compound interest in a cumulative value is often used for another purpose entirely: to measure the relative growth in such things as an investment portfolio or the earnings of a given company. Although the objective is different, the arithmetic is exactly the same.

To illustrate this, let's assume that the income of a given company has grown from $23 million to $51 million over a five-year period, and a company analyst wants to compare this growth rate with that of the industry as a whole, which grew from $1,013 million to $1,978 million over the same period. Your first step is to divide 51 by 23, which equals 2.2174, and then find the 1/5 root of this by the process above. The answer is 1.173, which means that this growth is equivalent to a 17.3 percent annual compound rate. For the industry as a whole, you divide 1,978 by 1,013 and get 1.9526. The fifth root of this is 1.144, which is the equivalent of a 14.4 percent annual compound rate of growth.

Note that when you divide 51 by 23 in this case to get 2.2174, you have a precise analogy to $1.00 growing to $2.2174 in five years, and use exactly the same arithmetic to find the compound rate of interest that will produce this result. The same is true, of course, for the industry growth rate.

All this is very useful as a quick summary device for comparing relative growth trends, with just one number to represent the trend in any given series of data over any specified period of time. But you should be aware that this calculation is based on only the first and last values in the series, and ignores everything in between. Sometimes, when the interim values are quite divergent, this can be misleading, and more elaborate statistical analysis (based on a trend line fitted to the data) should be used to get the average growth rate based on the values for all the years in the given period.

DIFFERENT TIME PERIODS

All of our examples thus far have been based on annual rates for full-year periods, but it is very easy to adjust for other time periods as well. Remember our basic equation:

$$\text{Value} = (1 + \text{Rate})^N$$

Now, let's assume that you want to put this on a monthly basis, and that you are dealing with a 10 percent annual rate and a three-year period. In this case the monthly *Rate* equals 10/12 or 0.833 percent, equal to .00833 in ratio form. *N* becomes 3 times 12 or 36. So to find this accumulated value you multiply 1.00833 by itself 36 times (which is the same as taking 1.00833 to the 36th power) and your calculator tells you that the answer is 1.348. This exceeds the value of 1.331 shown previously because of the difference between monthly and annual compounding.

The same process can be followed for any time period. For interest compounded daily, for example, you would simply divide the annual rate (in ratio form) by 365 to get the *Rate* in the equation, and then multiply the number of years by 365 to get the value of *N*. From that point on, once again, the arithmetic is the same.

SUMMARY

The law of compound interest enters into many practical decisions in the business world, and every manager should be familiar with the simple arithmetic involved. Apart from the practical value of such knowledge, it leads to improved judgment in the evaluation of growth rates of all kinds, especially those projected into the future, which often enter into key business plans. Poor judgment here can lead to disastrous results.

Executives can sometimes be quite naive, in my experience, in accepting projections based on some compound growth rate, little realizing what this implies in terms of absolute growth as pointed out earlier in this chapter. The simple fact is that nothing grows for very long at any compound rate, and any projection of this kind should always be viewed with great caution and suspicion.

CHAPTER 4

CONVERTING FUTURE DOLLARS TO PRESENT VALUE

AS A BUSINESS executive, you are likely to become involved in the investment of corporate money, and thus concerned about what it will generate in expected return. This return usually takes the form of a stream of payments in future years, and it is very useful to be able to summarize them in a single figure. For this, you need to turn to a concept known as *present value.*

As an illustration, let's start by looking at the cumulative value of $1.00 compounded annually at 10 percent interest:

End Of Year	Value
0	1.00
1	1.10
2	1.21
3	1.33
4	1.46
5	1.61
6	1.77
7	1.95
8	2.14
9	2.36
10	2.59

Now, if you are willing to accept 10 percent interest as a fair return on money, you come to a very interesting conclusion: *All the numbers in this table are equal in value.* And that is a very profound finding indeed, because it enables you to equate money values at any point of time, a powerful analytical tool to help you answer a wide variety of questions.

In brief, what the table shows is this: Under the given interest rate assumption, payments of $1.33 after three years, or $1.95 after seven years, or $2.59 after ten years, are all equal in value—and that is the value of $1.00 today.

Today's value, $1.00 in this case, is called the *present value,* and the other values in the table are designated as *future values.* Thus the present value of a $2.59 payment after ten years is $1.00, and the future value of $1.00 after ten years is $2.59.

The table is based on $1.00 compounded. Suppose that you are dealing with other amounts, such as the present value of $1,000. It is very easy to make this translation. For example:

Question: What is the future value of $1,000 after ten years? *Answer: $2,590 (1,000 × 2.59).*

Question: What is the present value of a $2,590 payment after ten years? *Answer: $1,000 (2,590/2.59).*

Thus the table, based on a 10 percent interest rate, enables you to compute present and future values for any amount of money, over a ten-year period, by simple multiplication or division.

There is still another way to arrive at these answers, which may be easier to understand from a conceptual viewpoint. Whenever you specify the value of money in terms of any given interest rate, you automatically fix the current value to be assigned to each future dollar.

For example, with $1.00 compounding at a 10 percent interest rate to $2.59 after ten years, what is the present worth of $1.00 to be paid ten years from now? The answer: If $2.59 then is worth $1.00 now, it follows that $1.00 then is worth 1/2.59 or $0.39 now.

In our present example, a $1.00 payment ten years from now has a present value of 39 cents (or 38.61 cents, to be more exact). So if someone promises to pay you $1,000 in ten years, that person will be paying you in dollars worth only 38.61 cents in today's value, and therefore this future payment is worth only $386.10 in current value.

In computing present value, therefore, you get the same answer either way: (1) By dividing the future payment by the compounded value of $1.00, or (2) by multiplying the payment by the current value of each future dollar, which is the reciprocal of the compounded value. It should be noted, however, that the $2.59 figure used in these calculations has been rounded, and the answer would be more precise if it were carried to two more decimal places, which would be $2.5937.

STREAM OF PAYMENTS

It is equally simple to extend this concept to another very important application: how to measure the total value represented by a stream of payments over time. Let us assume, for example, that you can invest $1,000 and get the following payments in return:

End of Year	Payment
5	100
6	200
7	300
8	400
9	500
Total	1,500

You invest $1,000 and get $1,500 back. Is that a good deal? At this point, you don't have enough information to answer that question. The $1,500 total return in this case really tells you very little because it treats all of the payments, at different points of time, as though they were equal in value per dollar, which clearly they are not.

How, then, do you correct for this? Very easily, as the following table shows:

End of Year	Payment	$1.00 Compounded	P. Value $1.00	Present Value
5	100	1.61	.621	62
6	200	1.77	.565	113
7	300	1.95	.649	154
8	400	2.14	.467	187
9	500	2.36	.424	212
Total	1,500	—	—	728

As before, you compute the present value of these future payments by dividing each payment by the compounded value of a dollar at the same point of time (based here again on a 10 percent interest rate), or by multiplying the payment by the present value of each future dollar (reciprocal of the compounded figure).

When you sum up these present value figures, you get the total of $728 as the present value of the entire stream of payments; and when you compare this with the $1,000 investment, you see that this is a very bad deal indeed.

Let me stress again that the interest rate assumption is vital in this analysis, because the present value of any stream of payments will change with every change in the assumed interest rate.

SUMMARY

You have seen that just adding future payments can be quite misleading in terms of evaluating return. A dollar today is not the same as a dollar five years from now, and that is not the same as one ten years from now, in terms of true value.

To add these various dollar amounts is indeed like adding apples and oranges and lemons. To convert them to apples only, they must be converted to dollars of equal value. And this is precisely what is done through the present value analysis.

Needless to say, calculating the present value of a stream of future payments is a very familiar procedure to accountants and financial officers, and many executives see the results of their analysis and have a fair idea of what they mean. But not many, in my experience, really know how the analysis is conducted, and most are consequently vague as to its underlying rationale and precisely how the results should be interpreted.

Thus, if you have learned how to use present value analysis, you may be certain that you will have an advantage over most others in your grasp of this key concept. Further, you will understand the basic structure from which is derived something called the internal rate of return— perhaps the most powerful single figure in the business world.

CHAPTER 5

RETURN ON INVESTMENT: ALWAYS THE KEY QUESTION

A CENTRAL POLICY consideration for any company is how to invest its capital, whether in new plant, equipment, purchase of another company, or whatever. Most managers sooner or later get involved in this consideration, either in recommending some investment or in the decision-making process itself.

With few exceptions, the key question to be asked in relation to any investment is the expected return. If you spend this much money, how much can you expect to get back? It sounds like a very simple question, but the answer is not always as clear and easy as it might appear, and most companies are likely to have some fairly definite rules on how the answer should be developed in each case.

Perhaps the simplest approach is a *payback analysis*, which can be illustrated as follows: Let's assume the purchase of a $10,000 machine with an expected return in terms of greater efficiency and cost reduction as follows:

COST SAVINGS

Year	Amount	Cumulative
1	$3,000	$ 3,000
2	4,000	7,000
3	5,000	12,000
4	6,000	18,000

Now you ask, At what point do savings equal the $10,000 investment? Clearly that occurs in the third year. With $7,000 in savings in the first two years, at what point in the third year will the additional $3,000 be accrued? Assuming equal savings throughout the year, this will happen three-fifths of the way through the year based on the ratio 3,000/5,000. From this you conclude that the initial investment will be recovered in 2.6 years, which is the payback period. And the investment could be recommended on this basis, as having a 2.6-year payback.

While this is a relatively crude measure of return on investment, it is sometimes used, especially for purchases of equipment when there is a relatively short payback period, as in this example. The rationale is simply that the investment is so relatively small, and the return so fast, that nothing more is needed to justify the expenditure. From a practical viewpoint, this often makes good sense.

LIMITATIONS OF PAYBACK ANALYSIS

But clearly the payback period tells you only one thing about the return on investment, and should not be used to compare one investment with another in terms of relative return. It tells you nothing, for example, about return beyond the breakeven period, and hence nothing about total return. And it is self-evident, of course, that a given investment might have a faster payback than another but still be quite inferior in terms of total return.

This is a serious flaw, because companies do not have an unlimited amount of capital to invest, and normally they must choose each year among a wide range of potential opportunities. Hence top management needs some objective guideline in deciding which investments offer the best total return. In other words, it is not enough to know that a given investment offers a good return. The key question is how that return compares with others when only some investments must be chosen from a number of opportunities available.

To illustrate this, let's expand our machine example, and assume that there are two machines available and you must choose between the two. Each costs $10,000, but one has a four-year life and the other an eight-year life, with annual savings as follows:

COST SAVINGS

Year	No. 1	No. 2
1	$ 3,000	$ 1,000
2	4,000	2,000
3	5,000	3,000
4	6,000	4,000
5	—	5,000
6	—	5,000
7	—	4,000
8	—	2,000
Total	18,000	26,000

Now, the question is which machine offers the best return? While Machine No. 2 will give you more total dollars in savings, you cannot base your decision on this alone because it takes no account of the time value of money. As you learned in the chapter on present value, it is quite improper to add future dollars unless they are discounted by some interest rate to get their present value.

It is quite possible, of course, to assume some interest rate and get the present value of all these future dollars based on that assumption, and then compare the total for one machine against the other. While this is a valid procedure, it is not sufficient for your purposes here because each interest rate assumed will give you a different answer for the two machines, and there is no way of deciding which one to use for your comparison. Clearly, you are not looking for this multiplicity of answers, but rather for one unique solution.

Nevertheless, present value analysis may give you some clue as to how to proceed. Suppose the question is put this way: At what specific interest rate will all these future dollars of return, in terms of present value, be precisely equal to the amount invested? Now, this can be calculated for each machine, and these two interest rates can then be compared to see which represents the greater return.

INTERNAL RATE OF RETURN

The interest rate thus calculated is called the *internal rate of return,* and it provides a precise, unique solution to all problems of this type. In our example, the calculations appear in Table 5.1, where you see that the rate of return is 24.89 percent for Machine No. 1 and 23.10 percent for Machine No. 2.

It is clear from the table that these figures are correct, because when future dollars are discounted by the given percentage, they add to the $10,000 investment in each case.

So you may conclude, in this example, that although Machine No. 2 returns a good many more total dollars than Machine No. 1, it is slightly inferior in terms of net return on a present value basis. As a practical matter, of course, the two net returns are so nearly the same that either is a suitable choice from that viewpoint, and it is

TABLE 5.1

CALCULATING INTERNAL RATE OF RETURN

MACHINE NO. 1

Investment	10,000
Rate of Return	24.89%

Year	Value of $1	Annual Return	Present Value	Cumulative
0	1.0000	0	0	0
1	0.8007	3,000	2,402	2,402
2	0.6411	4,000	2,565	4,967
3	0.5134	5,000	2,567	7,534
4	0.4111	6,000	2,466	10,000
Total		18,000	10,000	

MACHINE NO. 2

Investment	10,000
Rate of Return	23.10%

Year	Value of $1	Annual Return	Present Value	Cumulative
0	1.0000	0	0	0
1	0.8123	1,000	812	812
2	0.6599	2,000	1,320	2,132
3	0.5360	3,000	1,608	3,740
4	0.4354	4,000	1,742	5,482
5	0.3537	5,000	1,769	7,251
6	0.2873	5,000	1,437	8,687
7	0.2334	4,000	934	9,621
8	0.1896	2,000	379	10,000
Total		26,000	10,000	

thus appropriate to make the decision on other factors of an intangible nature.

The only tricky thing about this procedure is that there is no simple formula for calculating the discount percentage in each case, and it must be determined by approximation. In this process, you start with an estimate of the percentage rate involved and compute the present value on that basis. Based on this result, you choose a better estimate and work out the values again; and so on and on until the total present value equals the original investment.

While this is quite tedious to do by hand, it is a very simple procedure with a proper calculator or computer program, with which all you need do is list the amount invested and the annual returns, with the machine doing all the rest of the work in a matter of seconds. But the concept itself is very uncomplicated. The *internal rate of return* is simply the percentage by which future returns must be discounted to precisely equal the amount invested. It is a unique figure in each case, quite clear in its meaning, easy to interpret and compare in terms of one investment versus another.

It is also a very ingenious concept. If you are able to take any investment and any pattern of returns, with an automatic adjustment for the time value of money, and convert it into one simple figure, you have the magic key to unlock many doors in practical business analysis, in an environment in which investment decisions are always important and are sometimes critical to the future of the enterprise.

This knowledge can be very helpful indeed throughout your business career. In my experience, most executives are familiar with the phrase *internal rate of return,* and from the words alone have a fair idea of what it means, but beyond that are quite fuzzy on its precise meaning and how it is calculated. This confusion can be a real handicap in any practical application of the concept.

OTHER EXAMPLES

Let's suppose that your corporation has the opportunity to acquire another company. The acquisition price is $10 million in cash, and the target company had a net income of $1 million in the year just ended. Your analysts tell you that it is conservative to estimate that the target company can increase its net income by $200,000 per annum for the next ten years. From this you project its net income as follows:

NET INCOME

Year	($000)
1	1,200
2	1,400
3	1,600
4	1,800
5	2,000
6	2,200
7	2,400
8	2,600
9	2,800
10	3,000

Your CEO has made it clear that no acquisition will be considered if the rate of return is less than the 15 percent that your own company earns on its stockholders' equity, which is a rational and fairly typical restraint. Now, the question is, Does the proposed acquisition qualify under this benchmark?

Using the procedure just explained, you find that the income figures shown above represent a 13.7 percent return on the $10 million investment, which falls short of your benchmark. But, on second thought, you will note that something has been omitted from the data that you have used: No residual value for the target company is shown after the ten-year period, and this is clearly wrong. Obviously, the company will not be worthless after ten years, but how do you put a specific value on it?

The usual practice is to assume that the company could be sold for some multiple of its net income in the tenth year, and then assign that value to the eleventh year. Under normal circumstances, a multiplier of 10 is quite reasonable and acceptable for an analysis of this type, which would give you a residual value of $30 million in this case.

Now, if you run your analysis again with this residual value added in the eleventh year, you will find that the rate of return is 22.7 percent, which is well above the 15 percent benchmark. All these calculations, with and without residual value, are shown in Table 5.2, from which you can verify the rate of return in each case.

You have been taken through this step by step to show the power of this procedure, and how easy it is to analyze a multimillion-dollar acquisition and then summarize the results in a single rate of return figure. But the usual cautions apply, of course, to any forecast data, and their relative accuracy is always a matter of judgment. But once the necessary assumptions have been made about future income of the target company and the multiplier to be used in fixing residual value, this simple mathematical model will complete the entire analysis.

The same procedure can be used to evaluate any investment, and many corporations will require that it be followed, with proper documentation, as backup material to be included with any capital fund request, whether it be for plant, equipment, or what have you.

One postscript should be added. In the acquisition example, the analysis was based on projected net income of the target company, and this may be appropriate when the rate of return is to be compared with the acquiring company's net income return on its own stockholders' equity. More often, however, management will want to see return measured in terms of net cash flow, which, of course, can be quite different from reported net income. In other words, in most investment decisions, management is asking: If we invest this much cash, what is the rate of return in net cash that will be returned to us? And that, clearly, is a very rational question.

TABLE 5.2

CALCULATING RATE OF RETURN ON ACQUISITION

Acquisition Analysis: No Residual Value

Investment	10,000
Rate of Return	13.69%

Year	Value of $1	Annual Return	Present Value	Cumulative
0	1.0000	0	0	0
1	0.8796	1,200	1,056	1,056
2	0.7737	1,400	1,083	2,139
3	0.6805	1,600	1,089	3,227
4	0.5986	1,800	1,077	4,305
5	0.5265	2,000	1,053	5,358
6	0.4631	2,200	1,019	6,377
7	0.4073	2,400	978	7,354
8	0.3583	2,600	932	8,286
9	0.3152	2,800	882	9,168
10	0.2772	3,000	832	10,000
Total		21,000	10,000	

Acquisition Analysis: With Residual Value

Investment	10,000
Rate of Return	22.71%

Year	Value of $1	Annual Return	Present Value	Cumulative
0	1.0000	0	0	0
1	0.8149	1,200	978	978
2	0.6641	1,400	930	1,908
3	0.5412	1,600	866	2,774
4	0.4411	1,800	794	3,568
5	0.3594	2,000	719	4,287
6	0.2929	2,200	644	4,931
7	0.2387	2,400	573	5,504
8	0.1945	2,600	506	6,010
9	0.1585	2,800	444	6,454
10	0.1292	3,000	388	6,841
11	0.1053	30,000	3,159	10,000
Total		51,000	10,000	

SUMMARY

Investment decisions are a major concern to top management and company directors, and are often quite complex. There is an obvious need for some technique that can summarize all these data, including related assumptions, in a single figure that can be readily understood.

Internal rate of return is such a device, and every manager should understand the concept, how it is calculated, and how it should be interpreted. A clear knowledge of this concept can be exceedingly useful in dealing with a wide variety of problems in the business world.

CHAPTER 6

FINANCIAL RATIOS: THE VITAL SIGNS OF A COMPANY

JUST AS A PHYSICIAN checks such things as your temperature, blood pressure, and pulse rate in examining your health, so do analysts look at financial ratios in testing the health, vitality, and strength of a company. All managers should have some familiarity with these vital signs and what they mean.

A ratio, of course, is nothing more than one number divided by another, a simple process, but one with a very powerful property. The resulting figure is an abstraction, divorced from the two numbers involved, and thus becomes comparable with other such ratios irrespective of the size of those numbers. To illustrate this, suppose you know the number of highway accidents in New York and in Virginia for some given time period. What does this tell you about relative highway safety in the two states? The answer, clearly, is that it tells you very little. The two states differ materially in size and traffic volume, and it is to be expected that total accidents would be much greater in the larger state.

In order to throw some light on the question of relative highway safety in the two states, you need to introduce another factor: miles traveled on the highways in each state. Now, if you divide the number of accidents by the miles traveled in each case, you get a ratio such as accidents per 100,000 miles traveled, and this ratio should be comparable from one state to another.

This is a frequently used procedure in analyzing data. Very often the raw numbers, because of size differences, can tell you very little, whereas ratios of those numbers, by contrast, can be highly meaningful. So it is with financial ratios in the business world. They are really quite easy to understand, and they tell a most interesting story in quick, succinct form.

For the purposes of this discussion, let's assume Company X has the very simplified income statement and balance sheet shown in Table 6.1. All our ratios will be derived from the figures in this table. Figures are shown in the table in thousands, and they will be expressed the same way in the discussion that follows.

LIQUIDITY RATIOS

First of all, let's look at two ratios of prime concern to those who extend credit or make loans to a given company. Both are concerned with the ability of the company to meet its immediate obligations. If you were a loan officer at a bank, this is certainly one of the things you would want to check before approving a short-term loan to the company. The same would be true, of course, if you were the credit manager of a supplier that was asked to extend a major line of credit to the company.

The first of these two ratios is called the *current ratio* and is simply current assets divided by current liabilities. For Company X, this is 350/250 = 1.4. In other words, for every dollar of current liabilities there is $1.40 in current assets.

Remember that what is shown on the balance sheet as current liabilities are those obligations coming due in the next twelve months, and what is shown as current assets are assets that should be convertible into cash in the

TABLE 6.1

INCOME STATEMENT
(In Thousands of Dollars)

Sales		800
Expenses		700
Interest	$ 50	
Depreciation	80	
All Other	570	
Operating Profit		100
Taxes		40
Net Income		60

BALANCE SHEET

Current Assets		350
Accounts Receivable	80	
Inventory	250	
All Other	20	
Fixed Assets (Net)		800
Total Assets		1,150
Current Liabilities		250
Long-term Debt		400
Stockholders' Equity		500
Common Stock	100	
Retained Earnings	400	
Total Liabilities and Equity		1,150

(Note: 20,000 shares outstanding)

same time period. So a ratio of 1.4 means that Company X should have more than enough cash to meet its immediate obligations.

At one time, there was a rule of thumb that the current ratio should be at least 2 to provide the proper margin of safety, but in actuality the ratio tends to vary by type of business (and perhaps by season of the year), so it may well be that 1.4 is completely adequate for Company X.

This illustrates the key point that financial ratios, like all statistical data, require proper interpretation. Everything is relative in the financial world, and there are no absolute norms. Deviations can and do occur, often for very sound reasons. Here is where the skilled analyst plays a key role. There is no substitute for thorough knowledge of the subject and sound judgment.

The next ratio to be considered in a liquidity analysis is the *quick ratio,* which is current assets minus inventory divided by current liabilities. For Company X, this is (350 − 250)/250 = 100/250 = 0.4. Here the concept is that a company in real trouble, facing bankruptcy, may realize very little if any cash from its inventory to meet the demands of its creditors, so value of the inventory is deducted from current assets accordingly in computing this ratio.

The old rule of thumb was that a company should have a current ratio of at least 2 and a quick ratio of at least 1 for its creditors to be completely happy, and clearly Company X falls considerably short of this in both ratios. The quick ratio of only 0.4, in particular, would appear to be very low indeed.

Whether this is a real problem would depend again on the circumstances: on industry standards, company background and history, quality of inventory, sales demand, and so on. With full knowledge of such circumstances, one might well find that the substandard quick ratio is acceptable; but certainly it flies a red danger flag that calls for investigation.

One other point that should be made here is that a

financial ratio based on a given income statement and balance sheet is a snapshot at one point in time. But this is a dynamic world and to understand fully what is happening you typically need to supplement that snapshot with a trend analysis of changes that have occurred over time.

Look at Figure 6.1. The current ratio of Company X appears to be quite acceptable at the end of the period if you consider that period alone, but the downward trend over the last six years, especially in contrast with the industry average, is clear cause for concern. What is the underlying reason for the steady deterioration in the current ratio in this company, and what is being done to correct the situation?

It is obvious from this why analysts want to see financial ratios for at least five years in the past, and preferably for

Figure 6.1

Comparing the Current Ratio of Company X with the Industry Average

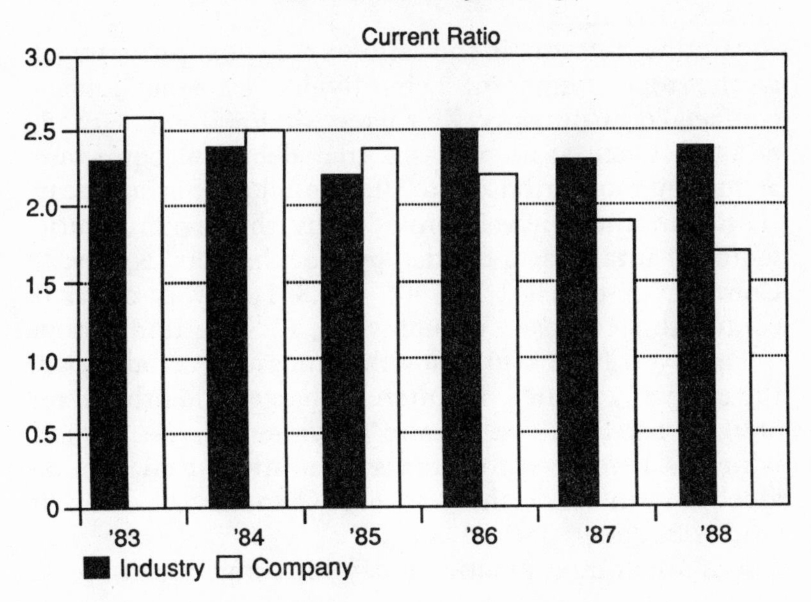

an even longer period, to get a clear picture of the dynamics involved. Here is a case in which the motion picture can be quite superior to a snapshot of the subject.

DEBT AND RELATED RATIOS

The next ratios you should consider are those of primary interest to long-term lenders and stockholders of a company, in terms of its debt load and relative security over time. The first of these ratios is *debt to total assets,* in which total long-term debt is divided by total assets. For Company X this is 400/1,150 = 0.348 or 34.8 percent.

A similar measure is *debt to total capitalization,* which is the total long-term debt divided by stockholders' equity plus the long-term debt. For Company X this is 400/(500 + 400) = 400/900 = 0.444 or 44.4 percent. The concept here is that the capital a company has to work with is provided by its own stockholders (plus retained earnings) and by money borrowed from long-term lenders, and this ratio measures the percentage of capital that is so borrowed.

Another measure is the ratio of *debt to equity,* which is the total long-term debt divided by stockholders' equity. For Company X, this is 400/500 = 0.8 or 80 percent. Once again you see that debt and equity are about equal contributors to the capital of this company.

Still another view is provided by the *leverage ratio,* which is total assets divided by stockholders' equity. In Company X this is 1,150/500 = 2.3. For every dollar of equity, this company is supporting $2.30 in total assets.

Then you have two ratios that measure the ability of the company to meet its interest charges and other fixed obligations. First is the ratio of *times interest earned,* which is income before taxes plus interest charges divided by interest charges. For Company X, this is (100 + 50)/50 = 150/50 = 3.

It is a common practice today for companies to lease

plant and equipment, and the rental to be paid can be a major long-term obligation. To take this into account, there is another ratio: *fixed charge coverage,* which is income available to meet fixed charges divided by fixed charges. Here the income available is measured by income before taxes plus interest charges plus lease obligations. If Company X had lease obligations of $50 (not shown in Table 6.1), then its ratio would be (100 + 50 + 50)/(50 + 50) = 200/100 = 2.

All of these ratios are clearly significant to banks and other lenders as well as investors and others interested in the long-term welfare of the company.

ACTIVITY RATIOS

Now we come to several ratios that summarize various operational aspects of a company. First among these is *inventory turnover,* which is total sales divided by the total value of inventory. For Company X, this is 800/250 = 3.2. This ratio will vary by type of business, and to gauge the significance of this 3.2 number, it should be compared with the industry average. In general, however, it is cause for concern if this ratio is too low, indicating that too much money is being tied up in inventory in relation to sales volume. Many small companies, in particular, have come to grief through failure to recognize this danger signal.

The next ratio is *average collection period,* which is the total of accounts receivable divided by sales per day. With Company X, this is 80/(800/365) = 80/2.192 = 36. This indicates that an average of 36 days is required to collect the receivables, and this figure must be interpreted in relation to the normal collection period for the company. If accounts are supposed to be paid in 30 days, for example, the 36-day average is a very good ratio.

If the average collection period is too high, by contrast, it is another danger signal. When customers are slow in paying their bills, many may not pay at all. Typically, the longer the age of an overdue account, the greater the risk that it will prove to be uncollectible. Again, many companies, and especially smaller ones, have found themselves in deep trouble through failure to recognize this simple principle.

Another ratio is *sales to fixed assets,* or sales divided by fixed assets. For Company X, this is 800/800 = 1. For many companies, certainly, this would be a very low ratio. Normally, you would expect to see far more sales per dollar of fixed assets; but once again, this ratio should be compared with the industry average for a more precise understanding of what it signifies. Clearly there is a vast difference, for example, between a manufacturing company with heavy investment in plant and facilities and a retailer who may rent space and have a minimum of investment in fixed assets.

Finally, there is the ratio of *total asset turnover,* which is sales divided by total assets. For Company X, this is 800/1,150 = .696 or 69.6 percent. The typical problem occurs when this ratio is too low but here, once again, it should be compared with the industry average.

PROFIT RATIOS

Now we come to ratios relating to profit, of central interest to security analysts, stockholders, and investors. The first of these is *profit margin on sales,* which is simply net income divided by total sales. For Company X, this is 60/800 = .075 or 7.5 percent, and once again this ratio should be interpreted in relation to the industry average, because profit margin varies widely by type of business. A 3 percent profit margin might be considered a superior return, for example, among chain food stores, but would be judged to be pathetically low for a jewelry retailer or a drug manufacturer.

A food store chain offsets its low profit margin by high

volume and high turnover of inventory and low investment in plant and equipment, all of which may be the exact opposite of, for example, a manufacturer of capital goods. In any event, the danger of a low profit margin is altogether evident; it has only a short distance to go to hit zero or beyond that to hit a negative figure. It is not very comfortable to be skating this close to breakeven or to a loss operation.

The next ratio, of special interest to stockholders, is the *return on net worth,* which is net income divided by stockholders' equity. For Company X, this is 60/500 = 0.12 or 12 percent. Again, while there is no absolute norm, a 15 percent return on net worth is generally considered to be quite satisfactory, and Company X is fairly close to that norm.

If only one ratio could be chosen to measure the overall performance of management, the return on net worth might be selected, and top executives accordingly view it with a great deal of interest. For stockholders, it is the measure of how well the corporation is using the capital they have provided, either directly or indirectly in the form of retained earnings. Sooner or later, either in dividends or higher stock prices or both, the stockholder hopes to cash in on this company return on his investment.

Finally, we have *return on total assets,* which may be measured in two ways: first, net income divided by total assets, which in Company X is 60/1,150 = 0.052 or 5.2 percent; second, net income plus after-tax interest divided by total assets, which in Company X is (60 + 50)/1,150 = 0.095 or 9.5 percent. The rationale for the latter procedure is that total assets include debt, and thus after-tax interest should be added to net income to make up the numerator in the ratio.

PRICE RATIOS

Next there are three ratios designed to measure whether a given stock price is relatively high or low. First and most widely used is the *P/E ratio,* which is the price per share divided by earnings per share (net income divided by number of shares outstanding). For Company X, assuming a stock price of $40 per share, the P/E ratio is 40/3 = 13.3.

To interpret this ratio, it should be compared with several things: the P/E ratio of the stock market as a whole, of other companies in the same industry, and of the company itself in years past. All of this information is readily available in various publications, including those of the Financial Services Division of Media General.

A comparison of this type will usually indicate whether a given stock price is relatively high or low, and the next step for the stock analyst is to try to understand why the deviation exists. The ideal, of course, is to find stocks that are undervalued by the market and thus have potential gains for an investor.

There is, however, quite a dispute on this measure of value in the academic world, where many hold to the theory of an efficient market, which maintains that everything worth knowing about a company is already known and fully expressed in the current stock price. Needless to say, most analysts on Wall Street, and many members of company management, take rather violent exception to this theory.

A related ratio, considered superior by many analysts, is *price to cash flow* (stock price per share divided by cash flow per share). Chapter 9 in this book is devoted to the subject of cash flow, and suffice it to say, for our purposes here, that cash flow for Company X is the sum of net income and depreciation. When put on a per-share basis, the ratio for the company is 40/(3 + 4) = 40/7 = 5.7. In this case, therefore, we have a stock price that may appear to be a little high in terms of its P/E ratio and yet appears to be quite low in its ratio to cash flow. Whatever the final judgment on this may be, calculation of the second ratio is clearly helpful in throwing more light on the subject.

A third ratio is *price to book value,* or the price per share divided by book value per share, which for Company X is 40/25 = 1.6. You will recall that book value is another term for net worth or stockholders' equity, or the difference between total assets and total liabilities. If a company were liquidated and realized the exact value of its assets as reflected in its balance sheet, and paid off all its liabilities as listed therein, this would be the value remaining for stockholders.

A significant part of book value can consist of fixed and other assets that are reported on a cost less depreciation basis, and these historic cost values may be quite different from current values. Because of inflation they very often understate current values, and for this and other reasons it is quite common for a stock price to be well in excess of the book value for a given company. Nevertheless, this third measure is useful when considered with the other two ratios in any analysis of the very complex question of whether any given stock price should be considered relatively high or low.

DIVIDEND RATIOS

Finally we have two ratios of prime interest to stockholders and investors interested in dividends paid by a given company. The first is *dividend yield,* which is simply the annual dividend rate divided by the stock price. If we assume an annual dividend rate of $1.20 by Company X, then this ratio is 1.20/40 = 0.03 or 3 percent.

The next ratio is *dividend payout,* which is the annual dividend rate divided by earnings per share. For Company X, this is 1.20/3 = 0.40 = 40 percent. It indicates that the company is paying 40 percent of its earnings to stockholders in the form of cash dividends, retaining 60 percent for company needs.

Investors or stockholders in a company are looking for a return on their investment in two ways: (1) in the ultimate gain they may make when they sell the stock, through an improvement in the stock price; and (2) in cash dividends along the way. Investors typically will differ in the weight attached to each of these elements. A retired individual, for example, may be primarily interested in protection of principal and a high cash dividend yield to meet current expenses. Someone else, by contrast, may have little interest in current income, and is seeking long-term capital gains when the stock is finally sold. In each case, the investor will search for companies that match these objectives.

A fully mature company, such as a utility, may be required to pay a large percentage of its earnings in dividends, with a corresponding high dividend yield, in order to attract investors with primary interest in current income. A new growth company in the technological area, by contrast, may pay no dividends at all, because it needs to retain all of its earnings to meet its growing capital needs.

Most companies will fall somewhere between these two extremes, but the dividend yield and dividend payout ratios are very good clues as to how the management of any company feels about its growth potential, and the type of stockholder that it expects to attract. All this is discussed in more detail in Chapter 15, on dividends.

SUMMARY

Financial ratios are indeed the vital signs of a company. They are easy to compute and their meaning is quite clear, but their full interpretation requires knowledge of the industry and sound judgment, just as a physician runs many tests but must apply his overall medical judgment in evaluating the health of an individual.

It is useful for any executive to have some grasp of this subject, and to understand how these simple ratios can sometimes fly a red danger signal for any company, and why top managers must heed them accordingly.

Table 6.2 is a summary of all the financial ratios discussed in this chapter, and shows at a glance how each can be derived from the financial statements of any given company.

TABLE 6.2

FINANCIAL RATIOS

Ratio	Formula
Liquidity	
Current ratio	$\frac{\text{current assets}}{\text{current liabilities}}$
Quick ratio	$\frac{\text{current assets} - \text{inventory}}{\text{current liabilities}}$
Debt	
Debt to total assets	$\frac{\text{long-term debt}}{\text{total assets}}$
Debt to total capitalization	$\frac{\text{long-term debt}}{\text{long-term debt} + \text{stockholders' equity}}$
Debt to equity	$\frac{\text{long-term debt}}{\text{stockholders' equity}}$
Leverage	$\frac{\text{total assets}}{\text{stockholders' equity}}$
Times interest earned	$\frac{\text{income before taxes} + \text{interest}}{\text{interest charges}}$
Fixed charges coverage	$\frac{\text{income available to meet fixed charges}}{\text{fixed charges}}$
Activity	
Inventory turnover	$\frac{\text{total sales}}{\text{value of inventory}}$
Average collection period	$\frac{\text{total accounts receivable}}{\text{sales per day}}$
Sales to fixed assets	$\frac{\text{total sales}}{\text{fixed assets}}$
Total asset turnover	$\frac{\text{total sales}}{\text{total assets}}$

TABLE 6.2 (Continued)

FINANCIAL RATIOS

Ratio	Formula
Profit	
Profit margin on sales	$\frac{\text{net income}}{\text{total sales}}$
Return on net worth	$\frac{\text{net income}}{\text{stockholders' equity}}$
Return on assets (1)	$\frac{\text{net income}}{\text{total assets}}$
Return on assets (2)	$\frac{\text{net income + after-tax interest}}{\text{total assets}}$
Price	
P/E ratio	$\frac{\text{stock price per share}}{\text{earnings per share}}$
Price to cash flow	$\frac{\text{stock price per share}}{\text{cash flow per share}}$
Price to book value	$\frac{\text{stock price per share}}{\text{net worth per share}}$
Dividend	
Dividend yield	$\frac{\text{annual dividend rate}}{\text{stock price per share}}$
Dividend payout	$\frac{\text{annual dividend rate}}{\text{earnings per share}}$

CHAPTER 7

BUILDING A BUDGET: HOW AND WHY

SUPPOSE YOU HAVE just been named assistant manager of your department and are properly prepared to meet the challenges of the new job. But after a week or so, the manager calls you into his office and says: "By the way, in addition to your other duties, you are also responsible for preparing the annual budget for the department, which must be completed by such and such a date."

If you are like most of us, your reaction to this announcement is likely to be a good deal less than joyous. You don't know much about budgets, but your general impression is that they are, at best, some kind of necessary evil to be avoided if at all possible. If you do have this initial prejudice, I would suggest that you put it aside and approach your new assignment in a constructive spirit. In so doing, here are some of the rules and guidelines to keep in mind.

Every company, whether large or small, needs to plan. It must anticipate what will be needed in supplies and materials, manpower and capital, and make arrangements accordingly. Anyone with business experience knows that it is dangerous to assume that the future will take care of itself. Proceed on that basis and you court disaster at every turn.

Most managers get involved in the budget-making process at one time or another. Although tedious, it is not an esoteric procedure, and the rules of good budgeting are based essentially on common sense and sound business judgment.

Typically, a budget is drawn up for an annual period, and the logical first step is to look at actual expenditures and revenues for the previous year. With a good accounting system, expenditures for the prior year will be broken down and reported in considerable detail on a line by line item basis. Because many expenditures tend to vary with volume of production or sales, it makes sense to start with an estimate of these elements. This may be the most critical part of the entire budget, and a good manager will solicit all the advice he can get from his sales and marketing people.

Many things must be considered in a sales forecast, including the economic environment, pricing, competitive forces, and changes in share of market. All this finally comes down to a matter of judgment, and how well this judgment is exercised is a major determinant of how the budget will work out in actual practice.

The next step, based on the estimated production or sales volume, is to estimate the expenditures for the new budget on a line by line item basis. Here, again, it is helpful to look at the budget in terms of change from the prior year. For each line item, if the budget is above or below the prior year, what is the rationale for the specific change that is indicated?

Wages and salaries, for example, tend to be a large item in most budgets, and if the budgeted total is above the prior year, what is the explanation? If more people are included in the budget, what will they do and what will it cost? How much of the increase is due to higher wage and salary rates, and what is the percentage increase involved? Answers to questions such as these should be provided in any good budget. All significant changes in the operating environment should be noted. If, for example, a new branch office is to be opened, a separate, detailed exhibit on the extra expense involved should be prepared and attached to the budget document.

Final budget figures for the year are typically broken down by individual month in the year, and the effect of seasonal variation must be taken into account for all the elements in the budget, with special emphasis on production and sales volume. Once again, the prior year can serve as a useful guide, but it should be recognized that this is not always reliable with special events and holidays. The varying dates of Easter, for example, can be a major problem for retailers.

Beyond this, in using the prior year as a guide, you should consider any abnormalities in that year caused by strikes or unusual weather or any other condition that may have distorted the normal seasonal pattern. So careful judgment is involved here as well.

From all of this, it is evident that considerable latitude exists for a manager to err on the conservative or the optimistic side in making up his budget forecasts, depending on his temperament and the way that budgets are viewed in the company. The natural tendency for any manager, who knows that his performance will be measured against the budget, is to underestimate revenues and overestimate expenditures. And while he may rationalize this simply as "conservative" budgeting, it tends to defeat the real purpose of the budget process, which is to come up with the best possible estimate of what the future holds.

Companies that are really serious about the process will correct these tendencies to err in either direction through a careful budget review procedure, in which higher corporate officers examine each segment of the budget in detail and require an explanation of anything that seems inappropriate.

ACTION BY THE BOARD OF DIRECTORS

Typically, there is a final review of the budget by the top officers of the corporation, with any adjustment they may wish to make, and the budget is then submitted to the board of directors for final review. It would be most unusual for the board to involve itself in any detail of the budget, but it is always keenly interested in the overall result and especially the projected profit for the year. Thereafter, throughout the year, it is customary for reports to the board to show actual performance versus the budget and also versus performance in the prior year. So the budget becomes a very important yardstick by which the board measures how well its management is doing.

There are some dangers in this. I have served on various boards over a period of years, and it is very easy in my opinion for board members to put undue emphasis on these budget comparisons. For this reason, top management may sometimes strain too hard to meet budgetary goals, at the cost of longer-term and much more important criteria, and this attitude can spread throughout the entire company. This is foreign to what the concept "budget" really means. It is a planning tool, no more and no less. It can be a valuable tool, but circumstances change daily in the business world, often in a way that could not reasonably be anticipated, and even the best plan can quickly become obsolete.

When this happens, it is often better for the board and top management simply to recognize that overall budgetary goals have become meaningless and look for some other means by which to measure relative performance. But as obvious as this advice may seem, it is rarely followed in practice in my experience, and it is not unusual for top management to spend a good deal of valuable time at every board meeting in explaining why the budget comparisons are no longer appropriate. And that can go on month after month throughout the budget year.

Again, this procedure has some impact on executives throughout the company when top management is pressing hard to come as close as possible to budgetary goals even when it is evident that such goals have become altogether unrealistic. The relative impact will differ in each situation, but the net result is likely to be trouble up and down the line in terms of sound judgment and rational decision-making.

THE BEST OF BUDGETS CAN GO AWRY

A major reason that budgets go awry is error in estimating sales volume, which can create serious problems in interpretation if board members and executives don't fully appreciate the degree to which expenditure levels in the budget are tied to estimated volume. To get some insight into the subject, let's look at the following example (numbers are in thousands of dollars):

Item	Budget	Actual I	Actual II
Revenue	1,000	800	1,200
Expenses	900	820	980
Profit	100	−20	220

One may assume that both management and directors would be most unhappy with Scenario I and very pleased indeed with Scenario II. In the first case, performance was well under budget; in the second case, actual results were quite superior to the budget expectations.

Now, the odd thing is that this company may well have been right on its expense target in both cases, however disparate the expense totals and bottom-line results. To see how this could be, let's look at the same figures again, but this time with expenses broken down into variable and fixed categories (numbers are in thousands of dollars):

Item	Budget	Actual I	Actual II
Revenue	1,000	800	1,200
Expenses:	900	820	980
Variable	400	320	480
Fixed	500	500	500
Profit	100	−20	220

Here we see that while total expense varied from the budget in each of the scenarios listed, it is a very different story with the expense components. Both variable and fixed expenses, when viewed separately, were right on target! Fixed expenses remained the same at $500,000, and variable expenses were 40 percent of revenue in each case.

So the deviation in total expense is not really due to error in expense budgeting, but results entirely from the variation in estimated revenue. This is an important distinction that should be clearly understood by top management and the board of directors.

Unfortunately, this type of breakdown and analysis is rarely seen in budget comparisons, and they accordingly tend to be a mixed bag, making it very difficult to evaluate the true effect of revenue and expense deviations.

FLEXIBLE BUDGET

It is possible, of course, to follow the model above in the budgeting process itself and come up with a flexible budget, with variable expenses set not as some fixed amount, but rather as some ratio of revenue or sales volume, and then adjust expenditure totals in the budget accordingly month by month for comparison with actual figures.

In years past, this was strongly recommended by some experts in the field, and I once gave some thought to installing such a system, but finally decided that it was much too complex in actual practice. It would have been difficult to train all the people involved, and continue to train their replacements. And there was real doubt that line managers would ever feel comfortable with such a system.

So it was my conclusion that it was better to live with the usual budgeting process. While it had some clear deficiencies, it also had its merits. The process was familiar to everyone involved and no special training was required. And it was useful to a good manager in keeping an eye on expenses.

In brief, it seemed to me that the usual budget procedure, assuming proper interpretation of deviations from budget throughout the year, was reasonably effective in terms of expense control. Where it tended to fall apart, especially from a top-management viewpoint, was in its role as a profit forecasting device with the passage of each month in the budget year.

FORECAST LIMITATIONS

In the real world, it is exceedingly difficult to foresee at budget time all of the things that may happen in the forthcoming year, especially on the revenue side. Changes in the general economy, competitive activity and pricing, and a host of other factors can materially alter the initial revenue estimates, with significant impact on expected profit. Thus it has been, in my experience, that many budget profit projections became obsolete after only a few months of the budget period had passed, and it was quite useless, if not downright misleading, to compare them with actual profit totals being reported month by month thereafter.

In lieu of such comparisons, there was a clear need for profit forecasts that would adjust to these many changes each month throughout the year and be as accurate as current knowledge would permit. These forecasts should make use of expenditure data in the budget, but otherwise be quite independent of any initial budget projections of revenue.

All this seems quite simple to me now, but I remember that it was not that obvious at the time. All of us had been trained in the normal budgetary procedure. We were accustomed to making the usual comparisons with budget, always with the underlying assumption that the budget, once approved, must be considered as sacrosanct, not to be revised in any way. It was not easy to discard this concept and move in a very different direction.

But we were pushed in this direction because, like all managers, I knew that our operating results last month and year-to-date were pure history, over and done with. Quite often it was interesting history, but it had already been written and there was nothing anyone could do about it.

What we might be able to do something about was the future, the months yet to come in the budget year, but for this we needed a better and more reliable way to keep track of that future, using our best managerial talent and all our current knowledge of revenue trends and potential on a continuing basis.

We set up such a system and found that the combination of an annual budget to control expenditures, supplemented by current forecasting of sales volume, updated each month and translated into a revised profit forecast, was indeed a highly effective management tool. It required some time and effort, both at headquarters and at division level, but results fully justified the investment in executive effort. This procedure has now been in operation for many years and continues to be as useful as it was in the beginning.

SUMMARY

Budgeting is an essential device for expense control, but it should be understood that budget comparisons with actual data can be highly misleading due solely to changes in expected revenue.

In an ideal world, planners would know the composition of each expense item in terms of variable and fixed costs, but in the real world precise information is rarely available. Even so, it is useful to make the best possible estimate of this composition in order to evaluate how expenses can be expected to vary with sales or production volume.

In any event, managers who are involved in budgeting should recognize that it is not just another tedious exercise, but rather a valuable planning tool in any organization, sufficiently important to merit their full attention and best effort.

CHAPTER 8

WHAT PRO FORMAS REALLY MEAN

IN THE BUSINESS world, a *pro forma* is some kind of projection, usually one involving expected profit and loss in some venture or enterprise. Typically, past operating data, if any, will be shown, and then projected for perhaps five or ten years in the future.

At higher echelons, the pro forma is a very familiar device indeed. In my many years as a chief executive officer, I must have encountered hundreds of them in one form or another. Based on that experience, I came to several general conclusions about them:

1. Like any guess about what the future will bring, they are always based on assumptions, and it is quite essential that these assumptions be made altogether clear and explicit.
2. Be especially wary when the pro forma is prepared by or under the direction of the sponsor of the project. In such a context, it is only human nature to err in the direction of optimism.
3. No matter who prepares it, the typical pro forma is likely to misread the future by a considerable margin, due to unforeseen circumstances well beyond anyone's initial vision or control.

Even with these qualifications, however, the pro forma

remains a useful and often an essential device. Although it is based on judgment, the pro forma requires that this judgment be put in quantitative form, along with its net effect, so that it can be evaluated accordingly.

If you are given the responsibility of preparing a pro forma on some new product or venture, you should be fully aware of all these considerations and be prepared for a properly skeptical review of your work by the top executives who must base their decision on what you have done.

SPECIFIC EXAMPLE

Suppose your company has a new product that it is ready to market, and you are asked to prepare a pro forma on the expected profit and loss for the first five years of operation. How do you go about this task?

The first step is to estimate the sales of the product, year by year, and the net price per unit, with sales times this unit price being equal to total revenue received. For this information you turn to your marketing department and solicit its help. Based on its knowledge of the market and the share of competitive brands, supplemented by market research, it will provide you with these key estimates:

Year	Unit Sales (In Thousands)	Price per Unit	Revenue (In Thousands of Dollars)
1	1,000	$3.50	3,500
2	1,200	3.60	4,320
3	1,300	3.70	4,810
4	1,400	3.80	5,320
5	1,500	3.90	5,850

Now that you have an estimate of sales and revenue, your next step is to develop corresponding estimates of the total cost of the operation, which breaks down into two major categories: (1) production, and (2) administrative and sales.

You recognize, first of all, that most costs have two components. The first component is fixed or overhead cost, which stays the same no matter what sales and production volume may be. The second component is variable cost, which, by contrast, does vary directly with such volume. Your cost estimates need to take that into account.

Beyond this, you must make some basic assumption about inflation. Will you build some rate of inflation into your cost estimates, year by year, or will you omit this and estimate all costs in terms of the current price level? Either choice is acceptable, but there is some merit in the assumption of no inflation. Estimates developed on this basis can later be adjusted, if desired, for any given rate of inflation that may be specified.

In this example, let's choose the no-inflation scenario. It is important, of course, that the estimated sales and unit price data be developed on the same basis, and we shall assume that this was the case with the estimates provided by the marketing department.

Now, in developing production costs, you go to the production manager and solicit his help. You explain that costs should be broken down by major category, and that they should be divided, when appropriate, into their fixed and variable components.

Salaries and wages represent a major item of expense, so the first task of the production manager is to determine the number of people that will be needed and the appropriate wage for each. This leads to an estimate of $516,000 per annum plus 32.7 cents per unit of production, with the former being the fixed or overhead element and the latter being the variable element of cost. For the production of one million units per annum, therefore, total wages and salaries are estimated at $516,000 plus .327(1,000,000), or $516,000 plus $327,000 for a total of $843,000.

The great advantage of breaking costs down into their fixed and variable components is that it makes it very easy to estimate cost for any level of production. In this case, for example, if production is specified at two million units per annum, wages and salaries are estimated at $516,000 plus .327(2,000,000), or $516,000 plus $654,000 for a total of $1,170,000. If this breakdown were not made, the only alternative would be for the production manager to redo his entire employment and wage rate analysis at each specified level of production, a very time-consuming and tedious process indeed.

Continuing with his analysis, the production manager estimates that employee benefits will cost $114,000 per annum plus 12.6 cents per unit of production. He also makes similar estimates for other categories of expense: materials needed, shipping costs, utilities, depreciation, and all other expense. In each case the estimate includes the annual fixed cost plus the incremental cost per unit except for depreciation, the annual charge for equipment and machinery needed to manufacture the product, which is estimated at a flat $150,000 per annum.

Your next step is to consult the chief administrative officer who will oversee the new operation, to get an estimate of sales and administrative expense. Here the major categories are salaries and commissions, employee benefits, advertising, supplies, rent, and all other. As before, these estimates are broken down into their fixed and variable components except for rent, which is estimated at a flat $172,000 per annum.

When you have obtained all this information, it can be summarized as in Table 8.1. With this information, and the estimated sales data, you can now put together the pro forma profit and loss statement shown in Table 8.2. To calculate the expense totals in each category each year, you simply multiply the variable factor times the unit volume of sales estimated for that year, and then add the fixed annual component for that item. All that

TABLE 8.1

COST ASSUMPTIONS IN PRO FORMA

Item	Cost Equation
Production Expense	
Salaries and wages	516 + .327(S)
Employee benefits	114 + .126(S)
Materials	127 + .672(S)
Shipping	52 + .107(S)
Utilities	31 + .042(S)
Depreciation	150
All other	75 + .150(S)
Sales and Administrative Expense	
Rent	172
Salaries and commissions	415 + .156(S)
Employee benefits	119 + .041(S)
Advertising	70 + .100(S)
Supplies	100 + .020(S)
All other	120 + .140(S)

ILLUSTRATION: If sales are 1,000 then production salaries and wages are 516 + .327(1,000) = 843. With all units expressed in thousands, this is equal to $843,000.

remains is to add the expense figures and subtract that total from revenue to get the expected profit or loss.

In this example, the operation begins with a $442,000 loss, which is converted to breakeven in the second year, and then builds to a $968,000 profit in the fifth year: fairly typical for a new venture of this kind. A great deal of information is compressed in this simple pro forma statement and, with the expense table added as an appendix, it is in a very readable format for presentation to top management.

But those who look at a statement of this type are likely to have another question, which should be answered: What happens if sales are less or greater than the

TABLE 8.2

PRO FORMA PROFIT AND LOSS STATEMENT

(All Data Except Price in Thousands of Dollars)

Item	Year 1	Year 2	Year 3	Year 4	Year 5	Total
Unit Sales	1,000	1,200	1,300	1,400	1,500	6,400
Price per unit	3.50	3.60	3.70	3.80	3.90	
Revenue	3,500	4,320	4,810	5,320	5,850	23,800
Production Expense						
Salaries and wages	843	908	941	974	1,007	4,673
Employee benefits	240	265	278	290	303	1,376
Materials	799	933	1,001	1,068	1,135	4,936
Shipping	159	180	191	202	213	945
Utilities	73	81	86	90	94	424
Depreciation	150	150	150	150	150	750
All other	225	255	270	285	300	1,335
Total	2,489	2,774	2,916	3,059	3,201	14,439
Sales and Administrative Expense						
Rent	172	172	172	172	172	860
Salaries and commissions	571	602	618	633	649	3,073
Employee benefits	160	168	172	176	181	857
Advertising	170	190	200	210	220	990
Supplies	120	124	126	128	130	628
All other	260	288	302	316	330	1,496
Total	1,453	1,544	1,590	1,636	1,682	7,905
Total Expense	3,942	4,318	4,506	4,694	4,883	22,343
Profit	−442	2	304	626	968	1,457

NOTE: Numbers do not add to totals because of rounding.

projection on the original plan? In other words, what is the outlook on a worst-case and a best-case sales assumption? Based on estimates provided by the sales manager, and using the same worksheet process as before, the answer is summarized in Table 8.3 with full details in Tables 8.4 and 8.5.

In these tables you see that on a worst-sales-case basis, there will be losses in the first four years and a profit of only $160,000 in the fifth year, with a total loss of $2,019,000 for the five-year period as a whole. On a best-sales-case basis, by contrast, there will be a profit each year, rising to $1,371,000 by the fifth year, with a total profit of $3,438,000 for the five years as a whole.

SENSITIVITY ANALYSIS

While such projections are very helpful, clearly there are many alternatives that might be considered. For example, the analysis thus far has dealt with only one assumption about what the price per unit will be each year, and this projection may be in error as well. How is it possible to show the profit impact of an even greater variation in both elements, sales and price per unit?

The answer is in what is called a *sensitivity analysis,*

TABLE 8.3

WORST AND BEST CASE VERSUS PLAN

	Sales Units (in Thousands)			Profit (in Thousands of Dollars)		
Year	**Worst Case**	**Plan**	**Best Case**	**Worst Case**	**Plan**	**Best Case**
1	700	1,000	1,300	−928	−442	44
2	800	1,200	1,400	−686	2	346
3	900	1,300	1,500	−424	304	668
4	1,000	1,400	1,600	−142	626	1,009
5	1,100	1,500	1,700	160	968	1,371
Total	4,500	6,400	7,500	−2,019	1,457	3,438

NOTE: Numbers do not add to totals because of rounding.

TABLE 8.4

WORST SALES-CASE PROFIT PROJECTION

(All Data Except Price in Thousands)

Item	Year 1	Year 2	Year 3	Year 4	Year 5	Total
Unit Sales	700	800	900	1,000	1,100	4,500
Price per unit	3.50	3.60	3.70	3.80	3.90	
Revenue	2,450	2,880	3,330	3,800	4,290	16,750
Production Expense						
Salaries and wages	745	778	810	843	876	4,052
Employee benefits	202	215	227	240	253	1,137
Materials	597	665	732	799	866	3,659
Shipping	127	138	148	159	170	742
Utilities	60	65	69	73	77	344
Depreciation	150	150	150	150	150	750
All other	180	195	210	225	240	1,050
Total	2,062	2,204	2,347	2,489	2,631	11,733
Sales and Administrative Expense						
Rent	172	172	172	172	172	860
Salaries and commissions	524	540	555	571	587	2,777
Employee benefits	148	152	156	160	164	780
Advertising	140	150	160	170	180	800
Supplies	114	116	118	120	122	590
All other	218	232	246	260	274	1,230
Total	1,316	1,362	1,407	1,453	1,499	7,037
Total Expense	3,378	3,566	3,754	3,942	4,130	18,700
Profit	−928	−686	−424	−142	160	−2,019

where expected profit is shown for a wide combination of sales units and prices per unit. Such an analysis appears in Table 8.6. As the name of the analysis implies, it clearly shows the sensitivity of profit to variations in each of these key elements at any specified level of the

TABLE 8.5

BEST SALES-CASE PROFIT PROJECTION

(All Data Except Price in Thousands)

Item	Year 1	Year 2	Year 3	Year 4	Year 5	Total
Unit Sales	1,300	1,400	1,500	1,600	1,700	7,500
Price per unit	3.50	3.60	3.70	3.80	3.90	
Revenue	4,550	5,040	5,550	6,080	6,630	27,850
Production Expense						
Salaries and wages	941	974	1,007	1,039	1,072	5,033
Employee benefits	278	290	303	316	328	1,515
Materials	1,001	1,068	1,135	1,202	1,269	5,675
Shipping	191	202	213	223	234	1,063
Utilities	86	90	94	98	102	470
Depreciation	150	150	150	150	150	750
All other	270	285	300	315	330	1,500
Total	2,916	3,059	3,201	3,343	3,486	16,005
Sales and Administrative Expense						
Rent	172	172	172	172	172	860
Salaries and commissions	618	633	649	665	680	3,245
Employee benefits	172	176	181	185	189	903
Advertising	200	210	220	230	240	1,100
Supplies	126	128	130	132	134	650
All other	302	316	330	344	358	1,650
Total	1,590	1,636	1,682	1,727	1,773	8,408
Total Expense	4,506	4,694	4,884	5,071	5,259	24,413
Profit	44	346	668	1,009	1,371	3,438

other element. Clearly, a tremendous amount of information is condensed in this one table. Because an entire worksheet like that in Table 8.1 is required to develop each figure in the table, you may also conclude that such an analysis requires a tremendous amount of work. That

TABLE 8.6

SENSITIVITY ANALYSIS

Projected Profit (In Thousands of Dollars)

Unit Sales (in thousands)	Price per Unit										
	3.00	3.20	3.40	3.60	3.80	4.00	4.20	4.40	4.60	4.80	5.00
1,000	−942	−742	−542	−342	−142	58	258	458	658	858	1,058
1,100	−830	−610	−390	−170	50	270	490	710	930	1,150	1,370
1,200	−718	−478	−238	2	242	482	722	962	1,202	1,442	1,682
1,300	−606	−346	−86	174	434	694	954	1,214	1,474	1,734	1,994
1,400	−494	−214	66	346	626	906	1,186	1,466	1,746	2,026	2,306
1,500	−383	−83	218	518	818	1,118	1,418	1,718	2,017	2,318	2,618
1,600	−271	49	369	689	1,009	1,329	1,649	1,969	2,289	2,609	2,929
1,700	−159	181	521	861	1,201	1,541	1,881	2,221	2,561	2,901	3,241
1,800	−47	313	673	1,033	1,393	1,753	2,113	2,473	2,833	3,193	3,553
1,900	65	445	825	1,205	1,585	1,965	2,345	2,725	3,105	3,485	3,865
2,000	177	577	977	1,377	1,777	2,177	2,577	2,977	3,377	3,777	4,177

is quite correct, but there are easy ways to accomplish it.

There are a variety of *spreadsheet programs* available for computers that are specifically designed to produce all the tables shown in this chapter, and to do so very quickly with minimum effort on the part of the user. The entire sensitivity table, for example, with all of its calculations, can be created by the computer in a matter of minutes. Any company of any size is almost certain to have programs of this type, and people who know how to use them, so there should be no problem on that score.

But I would recommend that managers who have their own personal computers, or ready access to one, spend a little time learning how to do the job themselves. The spreadsheet is a powerful tool for many kinds of analysis, and it is a shame not to put it to work for you.

SUMMARY

All the tables presented in this chapter should be included in a pro forma presentation to top management, along with a narrative explanation of the procedure that was followed and a summary of the findings. Pro forma projections give management the basis for asking intelligent questions, weighing the probabilities involved, and making the final decision about whether to proceed with the project.

Many business decisions are based on pro formas of one kind or another, sometimes involving very large sums, and sometimes the future of the company itself, and all managers should be familiar with the procedures and principles involved in their preparation and interpretation.

But in actual practice in the business world, the sad fact is that many such projections are deficient in one way or another, often lacking clarity and proper detail in spelling out the key assumptions. Consequently, they are a poor basis for executive decision-making.

To be charged with the responsibility of preparing a pro forma, or to be involved in its preparation, is an important assignment for any manager. It can be a significant step in your career, and thus there is special reason for you to understand the guidelines that can help you do the job correctly.

CHAPTER 9

CASH FLOW: THE REAL TEST

HAVE YOU EVER read a news story about some company reporting a huge loss in a given fiscal year, and perhaps a similar loss for several years in a row, and wondered how such a company could possibly survive? The answer may surprise you. It is quite possible for a company to report losses such as this and still be quite solvent in terms of actual cash generated from operations. The reason is very simple. Charges are made against reported earnings that require no current cash outlay whatsoever, and this can make a major difference between earnings and cash flow. Here is an example:

INCOME STATEMENT FOR TWO CORPORATIONS
(In Thousands of Dollars)

Item	A	B
Revenue	$10,000	$10,000
Expenses	9,000	11,000
Administrative	5,000	4,000
Production	4,000	3,000
Depreciation	0	4,000
Operating Profit	1,000	−1,000
Cash Flow	1,000	3,000

Here Corporation A reports an operating profit of $1 million versus a net loss of $1 million for Corporation B, but the latter has a positive cash flow from operations of $3 million, or three times as much as the former. The difference, of course, is wholly in the depreciation item. The earnings of Corporation B are charged with $4 million in depreciation, producing a net operating loss for the year; but this is a bookkeeping charge only, which requires no current cash outlay of any kind, thus leading to the huge difference between reported operating profit and cash flow.

This is an exaggerated example, but the point made is quite valid and important. For purposes of simplicity, income taxes were not included in the table, but they would not alter the basic conclusion. Reported earnings may or may not be the best guide to the fiscal health of any company.

Accounting principles require the depreciation of investment in fixed plant and equipment over a period of years approximating the life of the fixed assets involved. This is sound procedure because it is presumed that these assets will have to be replaced at the end of their useful life, and it is appropriate to show a proper charge along the way. But however proper it may be, the fact remains that no cash outlay is involved.

The more a company has in fixed assets, the more important this becomes. A retailer, for example, may lease his floor space and even his fixtures, and thus have virtually no annual charge for depreciation. In a paper mill, by contrast, hundreds of millions of dollars may be invested in plant and equipment, and the depreciation charge can be equally substantial in relation to reported earnings.

TO BUY OR TO LEASE?

Whether to buy or lease equipment raises an interesting policy question for some companies. An airline company, for example, can borrow money and buy its airplanes, or it can lease the equipment. In the first case, earnings will be charged with interest on the loan plus depreciation of the equipment, and the two combined may be a good deal more than the cost of leasing the equipment as a charge against earnings. Thus, even though the purchase option may be the better of the two, in terms of real cost over time, the lease option may still produce a substantial improvement in reported earnings from year to year, and management cannot ignore this in making its decision.

Tax laws, of course, have a powerful effect on all such decisions. Depreciation allowances are useful to a company as a deduction in calculating income tax, and it has been a part of our tax policy to allow acceleration of these allowances to encourage capital investment, with a greater amount being permitted in the early years after the investment. Normally, in terms of true net cost to the company, this would favor the purchase rather than the leasing of equipment. But clearly it would not apply to companies that are unable to use the allowances because of insufficient or negative income. In these cases, the depreciation allowance in effect becomes worthless, and the lease option may become more attractive even though there can be no tax deduction for the lease payments.

In any event, cash flow is always a vital element to be considered by management and by others who are analyzing a given corporation. It should be noted, however, that the method we have shown for measuring cash flow is a short-cut approximation to a more precise analysis of all the elements involved. The approximation, which consists simply of adding depreciation to reported net income, is often used by analysts because it is quick and easy to compute and the necessary data are readily available. The more complete analysis, by contrast, requires data not normally available except through the complete audit of the corporation as shown in its annual report.

A MORE PRECISE ANALYSIS

An illustration of the various elements that enter into cash flow from operations is shown in Table 9.1, which is based on actual corporate data.

Here again you start with reported net income of $42.9 million as your base figure. To this you need to add four items that were deducted in arriving at the net income figure, but do not require a cash outlay: depreciation, provision for doubtful accounts, deferred income taxes, and increase in accrued expenses. In aggregate, these plus adjustments amount to $70 million.

Next you need to subtract those items that improved net income but provided no actual cash: increase in accounts receivable, increase in inventory, increase in other current assets, and decrease in accounts payable.

TABLE 9.1
CASH FLOW FROM OPERATIONS
(In Thousands of Dollars)

Net Income	42,900
Add	
Depreciation	41,500
Provision for doubtful accounts	13,500
Deferred income taxes	8,600
Increase in accrued expenses	6,400
Total	70,000
Deduct	
Increase in accounts receivable	22,800
Increase in inventory	2,800
Increase in other current assets	7,400
Decrease in accounts payable	2,500
Total	35,500
Net Change	34,500
Cash Flow Provided by Operations	77,400

All together, these items equal a deduction of $35.5 million from net income.

When all these adjustments are made to net income, the result is $77.4 million in cash provided by operations, somewhat less than the short-cut estimate of $84.4 million obtained simply by adding depreciation to net income; but the latter, in this case, is still a pretty fair approximation.

The key point, however, is that reported net income materially understates the cash flow in this corporation, and it can be an equally poor indicator in other companies. As a result, many analysts pay little or no attention to reported net income in placing a value on certain companies, preferring instead to work with some multiple of cash flow.

It is the usual practice, for example, in estimating the value of broadcast stations, where the typical approach is to use some multiple of cash flow, with the latter being given a rather odd definition: operating income before interest, depreciation, and taxes. At this point in time, for example, a ten-times multiple of this cash flow is a fairly common estimate of what a radio station should sell for.

CASH BUDGETS

Corporations must have cash to meet their various needs, and they must get it either from cash generated by operations or by borrowing or by additional equity from investors, so cash flow is a vital subject for corporate managers. Table 9.1 shows the key elements that should be kept under close scrutiny at all times.

The chargeoff rate for bad accounts can be a critical factor in some cases, with credit card companies a prime example. It is related, of course, to the policy on extension of credit and to the efficiency of the collection procedure.

Cash is tied up in accounts receivable, and well-managed companies will always work to keep them at a minimum, in relation to sales volume. The same is true, of course, of inventory. Excessive inventory is always costly in terms of the frozen cash involved.

One way that a company can preserve cash is to defer payment of its own bills. There is no point in paying bills before they are due, but there are clear dangers in going beyond this point in terms of credit impairment. Such a policy can also be costly if cash discounts are lost in the process. Even so, some companies resort to various stratagems, including finding some small fault with complex invoices, to stretch out their payments. The practice is particularly noticeable in recession periods, when many companies are severely pinched for enough cash to meet their operating needs.

It is obvious that a well-managed company, in addition to the usual budget, will have an equivalent cash budget as well. To be most useful, this cash budget will extend at least through the current year, and preferably several years into the future. It should start with cash generated from operations, and then take account of investments, capital outlays, debt payments, and new borrowing. The result is a financial blueprint of the future, which is vital to efficient corporate planning.

Neglect of cash flow considerations is no doubt a major factor in many corporate failures. Companies can grow too rapidly, for example, and fail to recognize that the cash needs for increased inventory, accounts receivable, and other elements of working capital have far outstripped their cash resources. Inadequate or improper financial control is always tempting fate in terms of corporate disaster.

SUMMARY

Reported net income of a corporation is a significant figure, but it can be and often is a poor indicator of the cash flow being generated by operations, which is needed to meet payrolls and pay bills. It is simple enough, by the methods explained in this chapter, to calculate the cash flow either with a quick approximation or a more precise analysis, and it is a worthwhile exercise for anyone studying the company.

Competent management will keep all elements of cash flow under constant surveillance and control, and will formalize its scrutiny with careful cash budgets well into the future. Failure to do so is an invitation to serious trouble and possible disaster.

CHAPTER 10

BREAKEVEN ANALYSIS: X-RAY OF ANY OPERATION

THE FIRST LAW of any business enterprise is to make a profit. Eliminate the profit for any period of time and the enterprise is likely to be eliminated as well. This being so, it is surprising how few managers have a clear view of the profit structure in their own company or division and the interplay of key elements in that structure. For all such managers, it will be highly instructive to make what is known as a *breakeven analysis*.

Breakeven analysis is a powerful analytical tool, simple in concept and easy to apply, whether you deal with one product, a single division, or an entire company. To illustrate this, let us assume the following operating results for a one-product division:

	Total	Per Unit
Units	100,000	—
Revenue	$1,000,000	$10.00
Expenses	800,000	8.00
Fixed	300,000	3.00
Variable	500,000	5.00
Profit	200,000	2.00

The first question is: At what level of unit sales is this division operating at breakeven, with losses below that level and profits above? To answer that question, note first that the marginal profit per unit is revenue less variable cost per unit (10 – 5) which is equal to $5.00. This is the marginal or incremental profit contribution for each additional unit sold.

Now, in order to break even, total fixed costs must be covered—$300,000 in this case. Thus, with marginal profit of $5 per unit, it requires the sale of 60,000 units to cover fixed costs, and this is the breakeven level of sales in this example.

So if you know your fixed costs and your marginal profit per unit, you simply divide the former by the latter to get the breakeven point of sales. No more complicated than that.

But there is a good deal more to be learned from a breakeven analysis, which can tell you not only the breakeven point itself, but also the profit or loss at any level of sales, which is simply the units sold times marginal profit per unit, less total fixed costs. In our example:

$$\text{Profit} = \$5 \times \text{Units} - \$300{,}000$$

Now you can prepare a table showing total profit at each unit level of sales:

Units	Profit
0	$–300,000
20,000	–200,000
40,000	–100,000
60,000	0
80,000	100,000
100,000	200,000
120,000	300,000
140,000	400,000

This analysis can easily be put into graphic form, of course, as shown in Figure 10.1, which has two key

Figure 10.1

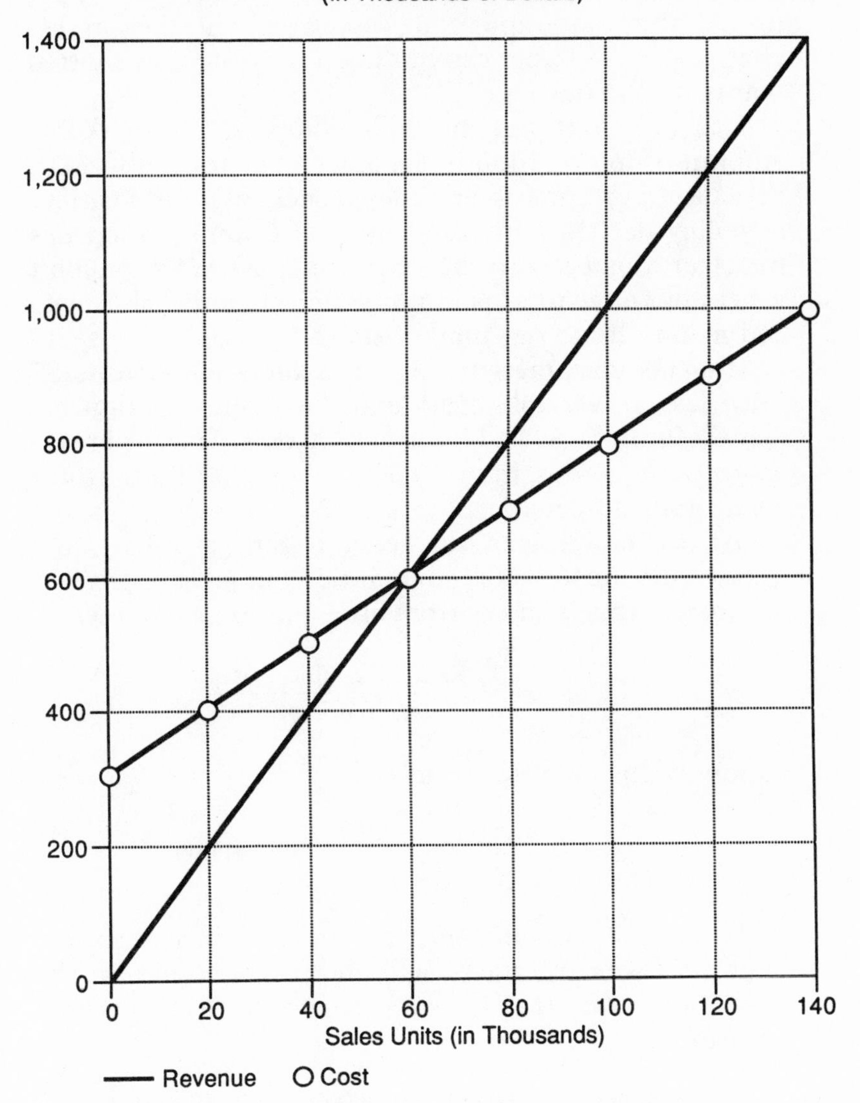
Breakeven Chart
(In Thousands of Dollars)
1,400
1,200
1,000
800
600
400
200
0
0
20
40
60
80
100
120
140
Sales Units (in Thousands)
Revenue
Cost

elements: in the cost line, the fixed cost total is the cost at zero sales level and the slope of the line (increase in cost per unit increase in sales) is the marginal cost per unit. Both revenue and total cost are straight lines on this chart, and thus either can be drawn from any two plotted points on the line.

Both the chart and the table compress a remarkable amount of information in succinct, easy-to-read format: very useful information for managers in making a variety of policy decisions. In this case, for example, the sales manager might say to the general manager: "Why don't we cut our price to $7 per unit, which should enable us to add materially to our market share?"

At $7 per unit, marginal profit becomes $2 per unit ($7 price less $5 variable cost), and the profit equation becomes: Profit = $2 × Units − $300,000. And the breakdown point jumps from 60,000 to 150,000 units (fixed costs divided by marginal profit).

"At this new price," the general manager asks, "how many units must we sell to maintain our present profit?" To answer this, you rewrite your equation as follows:

$$\text{Units} = \frac{\text{Profit} + \text{Variable Costs}}{\text{Marginal Profit}}$$

which in this case turns out to be:

$$\text{Units} = \frac{200{,}000 + 300{,}000}{2} = 250{,}000$$

"Now," the general manager continues, "what happens to profit if we continue to sell our present volume at the new price?" And this answer, going back to our original equation, is:

$$\text{Profit} = \$2 \times 100{,}000 - 300{,}000 = -100{,}000$$

Thus breakeven analysis serves to bring the price recommendation into very sharp perspective. At the new price, the breakeven point would go from 60,000 to 150,000 units. To maintain present profit, units sold must jump from 100,000 to 250,000. And if there were no sales increase, the $200,000 profit of the division would sink into a $100,000 loss. Needless to say, the latter contingency might well occur because, in the real world, competitors are not inclined to sit idly by while others cut prices to steal their customers.

Using the same formula, it is easy enough to construct a new table showing profit at various levels of unit sales with the new price and draw a new line accordingly on your breakeven chart. Breakeven analysis cannot of itself provide an answer to the price recommendation, but it does bring the consequences of that change into sharp focus as a basis for judgment and decision. Indeed, after seeing these results, the sales manager may well decide to withdraw his recommendation.

USING DOLLAR TOTALS

To illustrate the concept of breakeven analysis, we have used the simplest possible example of a one-product division. In actual practice, of course, things are likely to be a good deal more complicated, with a number of different products and a variety of profit margins within the mix.

In a complex situation of this kind, a precise analysis requires that each product be treated separately, but if you are willing to assume no change in the product mix, you can simplify the analysis considerably. To illustrate this, here is our example again with unit data eliminated:

Revenues	$1,000,000
Expenses	800,000
Fixed	300,000
Variable	500,000
Profit	200,000

Marginal profit (revenue less variable costs) is .50 (or 50 percent) of revenue. If you divide fixed costs by .50, you get $600,000 as the breakeven level of sales in dollars. The profit equation for any level of sales in dollars becomes: Profit = .5 × $Sales − Fixed Costs. From this you can draw another breakeven chart accordingly, replacing unit sales with dollar sales. How realistic this analysis may be depends on the accuracy of your basic assumption that the mix of products, and the profit margin of each, remains the same throughout the specified range in dollar sales.

In practice, it may be quite difficult to divide expenses into fixed and variable components. The guiding principle, of course, is that fixed costs are those that remain the same regardless of sales volume, which may be easy to define, but is sometimes far from easy to measure based on normal accounting data available.

There is, however, a statistical method for accomplishing this called *linear regression*, which can be used in a wide range of situations and can often be an effective approach. In this procedure, the relationship between cost and sales is estimated based on actual past data such as monthly totals for the last twelve months.

You can see how this procedure works in a simple chart, Figure 10.2, called a scatter diagram, on which you measure sales along the horizontal axis and cost along the vertical axis. For each month, draw a small circle where the two values for that month intersect. Now, draw a straight line that comes as close to the circles as possible. This is the average relationship between cost and sales.

The value on the vertical scale at the point where the straight line passes zero on the horizontal scale is total overhead (fixed cost). This is $500,000 in Figure 10.2. In other words, if sales were zero this cost would still exist. But bear in mind that this value relates to the time unit involved. If monthly data are used, as in this example, this is the fixed cost per month, which must be multi-

Figure 10.2
Scatter Diagram

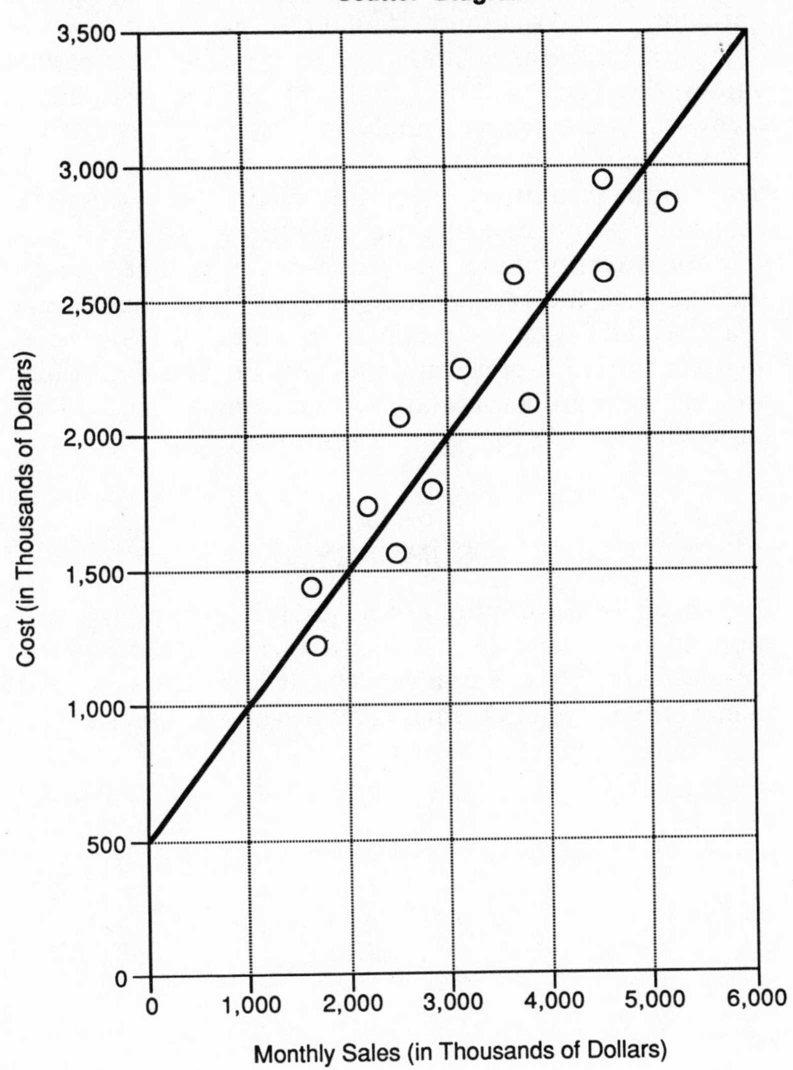

plied by 12 to get the annual total. The slope of the line—the increase in cost as sales increase by $1 on the horizontal scale—is the marginal cost per dollar of sales. In Figure 10.2, this is 0.50 or 50 percent. And these two values, fixed cost and marginal cost, are the basic ingredients for the breakeven analysis.

You might wish to make a breakeven analysis for your own company unit with a similar chart. Results may be very interesting indeed. The only thing added by the statistical technique of linear regression is that it picks the line with the best possible fit to all the circles on the chart, which may be some improvement over your visual approximation. If you want this greater precision, there are computer programs and even some small hand calculators that can do the job in a minute or two.

SUMMARY

Breakeven analysis provides a quick X-ray of any business operation and the key elements that determine the amount of profit at any level of unit or dollar sales. All managers can benefit from a knowledge of this technique.

CHAPTER 11

HOW TO SET PRICES

THE PROFIT OF any enterprise is dependent on the price it charges for each of its various products and services, and thus how to set the price in each case is always a major policy decision. In general, it may be assumed that most companies try to set their prices in such a way as to maximize their total profit potential over time. This sounds rational and simple enough, but it rarely works out to be this simple or easy in real-life situations where there are many complications to consider.

First of all, of course, are the variations by type of business. A department store has literally thousands of prices on the different items being sold, which is vastly different, for example, from a paper mill with only a single price on its main product. Clearly there is a similar difference in how the pricing process works in each case.

About the only sensible way that a department store can set prices is on a profit margin basis. If the goal is to earn a 40 percent profit margin, the cost of the item is simply divided by 100 – 40, or 60 percent, to get the indicated retail price. An item costing $12 would then be priced at $20 in order to get the desired markup. It is the responsibility of the buyer, of course, to select the item and determine how many units should be bought in the expectation that they will be sold at the indicated price and markup.

In a paper mill, by contrast, the manufacturer may have little discretion in setting a price for the product. For commodities such as this, there is generally an overall market price that will govern the maximum that any manufacturer can charge.

In general, the more individual the product, the greater the pricing discretion, which is one reason that manufacturers spend a great deal of money advertising their specific brands to try to establish a specific identity and market for each. To the extent that consumers can be persuaded that a given brand is separate and distinct from similar products, pricing flexibility is increased.

THE PRICING EQUATION

Two primary things must be considered in any pricing decision: (1) the cost of the product and (2) competition at each possible price level in terms of impact on sales volume. Again, in actual practice, it is a good deal easier to say this than it is to come up with the proper solution. But it is important, nevertheless, to understand how the analysis should proceed. To illustrate this, let's assume that your company has developed a new consumer product and made you its marketing manager. The product is sufficiently distinctive in its key characteristics to give you considerable pricing flexibility. How do you go about deciding what price to set?

Let's assume that careful test marketing has provided you with data on estimated demand at each price level, and that costs have been estimated at $150,000 overhead per annum plus direct or variable costs of $7 per unit. From this you can put together the figures as shown in Table 11.1.

Such a table can answer several key questions:

TABLE 11.1

HOW TO SELECT THE BEST PRICE

Unit Price	Unit Volume	Dollar Revenue	Cost			Profit
			Fixed	Direct	Total	
10	90,000	$900,000	$150,000	$630,000	$780,000	$120,000
11	82,900	911,900	150,000	580,300	730,300	181,600
12	75,600	907,200	150,000	529,200	679,200	228,000
13	68,100	885,300	150,000	476,700	626,700	258,600
14	60,400	845,600	150,000	422,800	572,800	272,800
15	52,500	787,500	150,000	367,500	517,500	270,000
16	44,400	710,400	150,000	310,800	460,800	249,600
17	36,100	613,700	150,000	252,700	402,700	211,000
18	27,600	496,800	150,000	193,200	343,200	153,600
19	18,900	359,100	150,000	132,300	282,300	76,800
20	10,000	200,000	150,000	70,000	220,000	−20,000

1. The largest demand in unit volume, at the lowest price of $10 per unit, is 90,000 units.
2. The largest dollar revenue is at $11 per unit for a unit volume of 82,900 and a dollar volume of $911,900.
3. The largest profit is at $14 per unit for a unit volume of 60,400 and a profit of $272,800.

So the price you select depends on what you are trying to accomplish. If you want to achieve the greatest share of market in unit volume, you will pick $10 as the unit price. This should enable you to sell the largest number of units, but your profit will be less than half of what could be earned at the $14 price.

If you are looking for the greatest share of market in terms of dollar volume, you will pick $11 as the unit price, but once again at a considerable sacrifice in terms of potential profit. And if you want to maximize profit, you will pick $14 as the unit price even though expected unit volume is a third less than its maximum potential.

Most of the time, you will be looking for maximum profit in a situation like this, but there are exceptions, especially with a new product, when there is great incentive to achieve a strong foothold in the market.

Here it may well be concluded that the sacrifice in potential profit is a reasonable price to pay to accomplish that goal.

But the key point is that the basic data provided in the table enables you to make a rational pricing decision and to understand its profit impact, whatever your marketing goal may be. Under ideal circumstances, every manager should be able to prepare a table such as this, summarizing the elements involved, before making any decision on prices.

PROBLEMS IN SETTING PRICES

Unfortunately, basic information of this type is not always readily available and not easy to estimate, especially the relationship between price and demand. For such a relationship to be valid, it must be assumed that all other things—advertising, distribution, and so on—remain constant. The reality, of course, is that this rarely happens. Constant change is the norm, rather than the exception, particularly with competitors and their changes in strategy.

What this means, in practice, is that most pricing decisions are made without the formal apparatus of a pricing table, but the fact remains that every such decision implies that such a table exists and that the given judgment is predicated on it. And the decision-making process might be much improved if some attempt were made, however crude, to estimate the data in such a table.

Many managers often miss the mark in the pricing process because they don't understand the hidden assumptions in the judgments they make. The great virtue of the pricing table is its requirement that all key assumptions be made explicit so everyone can see precisely what they represent and evaluate them accordingly. It is a very useful and valuable exercise.

Very early in my business life, I learned about this the hard way. I was persuaded, as a little side venture, to join several of my good friends in the purchase of a little company that manufactured a consumer product for sale in our local retail market. The investment was not large in total dollars, but it was nevertheless a fairly significant sum for me at the time.

The product being manufactured was clearly of high quality and well regarded by retailers in the area. Sales volume was brisk and growing. Employees were happy and morale was high. The general manager, who had developed the company, was bubbling with enthusiasm. And, along with the other new owners, I thought very well of my new investment.

As with many small companies, the financial report submitted at the monthly board meeting was prepared by an outside bookkeeper. It was a very abbreviated report, based mainly on cash receipts and expenditures, which didn't tell us much, except that sales and profits continued to grow, which we found very pleasing.

I did notice after a few months that, although our reported profit was increasing steadily, the same was not true of our bank balance. We always seemed to be short of cash. But our enthusiastic general manager was not concerned about this, and explained that the cash was being used for more raw material inventory and so on.

Then came the annual audit report, prepared by a CPA firm, and our little dream world collapsed in its cold pages. It appeared that all the fine profits reported by the bookkeeper were altogether fictitious, and the company had in fact operated at a considerable loss for the year. The reason was not hard to find. Our enthusiastic general manager had developed a standard cost for the product and, throughout the year, the monthly financial reports were based on the assumption that this was indeed the actual cost. The sad fact was that actual cost was a good deal more than this standard, so that reported profits were in fact actual losses.

And thus we began to understand why local retailers were so fond of our quality product. It was indeed a great bargain they were buying, at a price well below actual cost. No wonder that sales were going up at a rapid clip!

My partners and I decided that we had better try to recoup our investment by selling the company to someone with a greater knowledge of this type of business, and were fortunate to find someone who did, in time, turn it into a successful operation.

As silly as all this seemed in retrospect, it taught me a valuable lesson about the danger of pricing decisions based on false assumptions. I later learned that this is not just a hazard for small companies. Similar mistakes are made, all the time, by managers in very large and sophisticated corporations, often with very bad results.

SUMMARY

How a company sets the price for each of its products and services can have a material impact on its financial health and profitability and is a major policy concern.

Sound pricing decisions require a clear understanding of the fixed and variable costs involved and sound judgment on the relationship between price and expected sales volume.

The pricing table described in this chapter is a useful mathematical model of how all of these elements combine in terms of revenue and profitability. Preparation of such a table has the great virtue of spelling out, with total clarity, all of the key assumptions involved in the pricing decision.

CHAPTER 12

THE COMPETITIVE IMPACT OF OPERATING LEVERAGE

YOU SAW IN THE chapter on breakeven analysis how much could be learned about the operations of a company or division when cost was divided into its fixed and variable components. By the same process, you can get an insight into what is called operating leverage and its powerful impact on competitive pricing.

Operating leverage is the reduction that takes place in average cost with an increase in output. With output at so many units, total cost is defined as:

$$\text{Total Cost} = \text{Fixed Cost} + \text{Incremental Cost (Units)}$$

When you divide both sides of the equation by units of output, you get the equation for average cost per unit:

$$\text{Average Cost} = \frac{\text{Fixed Cost}}{\text{Units}} + \text{Incremental Cost}$$

For example, in a plant with $100,000 per annum in fixed expense and a variable or incremental cost of $10 per unit, the average cost at any level of output is:

$$\text{Average Cost} = \frac{100{,}000}{\text{Units}} + 10$$

Thus, if annual output is 10,000 units, average cost is 10 + 10 or $20 per unit. If annual output is doubled to 20,000 units, average cost drops to 5 + 10 or $15 per unit, and so on.

This simple equation makes the whole mechanism clear, and it is evident that as fixed cost is spread over more output, average cost will come down, but can never be less than incremental cost. Now, let's see what all this means in terms of economic reality.

This is illustrated in Table 12.1. Here you see output and cost figures for two plants, the first with fixed cost of $100,000 and incremental cost of $5.00 per unit, the second with fixed cost of $500,000 and incremental cost of $2.00 per unit. In the last two columns of the table, you see the average cost per unit at different levels of output. At a low level of output, Plant B has a higher average cost than Plant A, but at higher levels the opposite is true and Plant B has an increasing advantage

TABLE 12.1

OPERATING LEVERAGE AT WORK

	Total Cost		Average Cost	
Output (000)	**Plant A ($000)**	**Plant B ($000)**	**Plant A ($)**	**Plant B ($)**
50	350	600	7.00	12.00
100	600	700	6.00	7.00
150	850	800	5.67	5.33
200	1,100	900	5.50	4.50
250	1,350	1,000	5.40	4.00
300	1,600	1,100	5.33	3.67
350	1,850	1,200	5.29	3.43
400	2,100	1,300	5.25	3.25
450	2,350	1,400	5.22	3.11
500	2,600	1,500	5.20	3.00
Cost				
Fixed	100	500	—	—
Variable	—	—	5.00	2.00

over Plant A in average cost per unit. The operating leverage of both plants can also be shown graphically, as in Figure 12.1.

What this means, of course, is that Plant B at higher production levels can charge a lower price than Plant A and still make a profit. In addition, the higher the level of output, the greater this competitive advantage becomes. Faced with such ruinous price competition, Plant A may have no option but to close down, a victim of operating leverage.

Many parallels to this situation can be found in our economy. It is the fundamental reason, for example, that old steel mills in this country have been unable to compete with modern state-of-the-art mills in Japan. Heavy investment and high fixed cost in the latter are more than offset by greater efficiency in the form of lower incremental cost per ton.

Our example also illustrates the driving force behind the fight to increase share of market in order to raise the level of output because of the sharp reduction in average cost that can be achieved at higher levels of production. Indeed, the Japanese approach has often been to fight for share of market over an extended period, with little or no apparent regard for profit, in order to maintain a dominant position in the long-term market.

Operating leverage enters into competitive pricing in many ways. Consider, for example, a mill such as the following:

Percent of Capacity	Average Cost
60	$580
70	520
80	480
90	450
100	425

Figure 12.1

Operating Leverage
(In Average Cost per Unit)

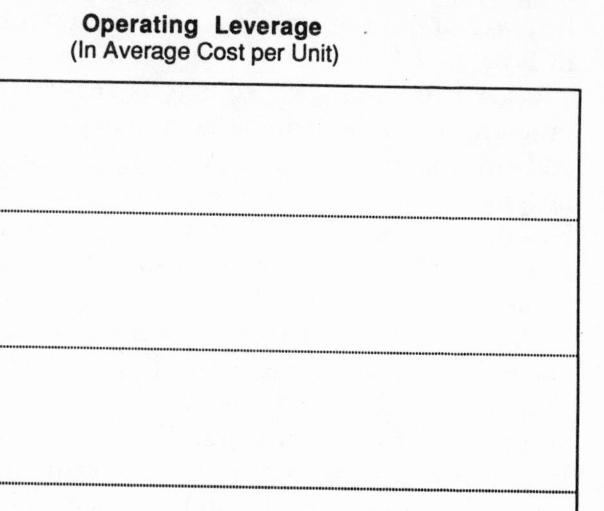

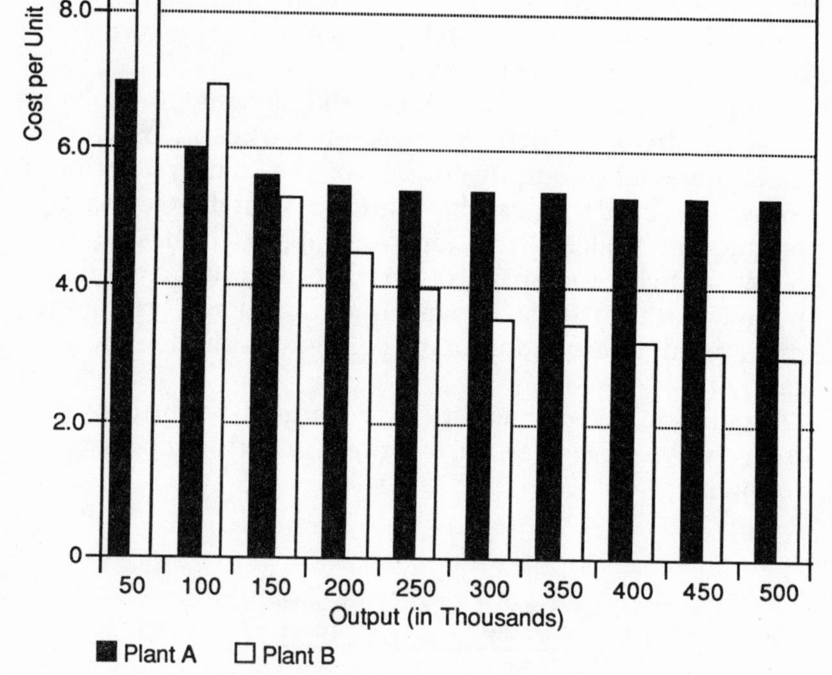

If the market price is $475 and this mill is operating at 80 percent capacity, then clearly it is losing money, because the price is not sufficient to cover average cost. In this situation, if the owners conclude that by reducing the price to a lower level, say $460, they can sell enough additional product to run at 100 percent capacity, they are very likely to do so in order to move from a loss to a profit position. Their action can, of course, generate similar action on the part of other producers, and if total market demand remains constant, the effort may well be self-defeating for all concerned.

This example is typical of those industries, such as the paper industry, in which the most efficient mode of operation is twenty-four hours a day, seven days a week. Typically, for such industries with heavy investment and high fixed cost, it is very inefficient to operate at anything less than full capacity, and it is to be expected that owners will make a maximum effort to sell enough product to make that possible.

Now, let's consider a variation of the above example. Suppose this mill is operating at 80 percent of capacity with an average cost of $480 per unit and a market price of $500, so the mill is making a profit of $20 per unit. The owners would like to sell the remaining capacity, but they conclude that a price cut would immediately be met by competitors and thus would be self-defeating.

But they also note that their incremental cost per unit is only $200, and they decide they should try to use their extra capacity to sell the product in overseas markets at a big discount. So they cut the overseas price to $300 (which is still a marginal profit of $100 per unit) and sell enough product to run at full capacity. Even with this huge reduction from the domestic price of $500, the net effect on profit is quite startling. Indeed, the total profit on this last 20 percent of capacity sold overseas at this seemingly giveaway price is greater than the domestic profit on 80 percent of capacity!

This process is known as dumping and although there

are laws against it, they are very difficult to enforce. The economics are clearly set forth in our example and are really quite simple. If a producer can recover all of his fixed and incremental cost and still make a profit in the domestic market, any sales beyond that in another market at any price above incremental cost will add to profit, no matter how steep the discount from the domestic price. It is easy to see why producers would find this practice very attractive and why those in the overseas market would find it equally unattractive.

The extra profit to be made in selling unused capacity at some price that exceeds incremental cost tends to be a key factor in many pricing decisions. Consider, for example, a television station with unsold time for spot commercials, or an airline with unsold seats on a given flight. The unused time or the unsold seat is worthless to the television station or the airline, and incremental cost is very nearly zero in each case. Thus there is great incentive to sell the time or the airline seat at a much reduced rate if this can be accomplished without destroying the general rate schedule. In terms of basic economics, of course, it is simply another form of dumping.

In all these examples, the problem of the company is how to maximize total profit and, if discounting is chosen to sell unused capacity at some price in excess of marginal cost, how to do so without spoiling the regular or normal market for the product. It is a very practical question for many companies, with considerable impact on their overall profit position.

SUMMARY

Operating leverage is the reduction in average cost that takes place with increasing output, as fixed cost is spread over a greater number of units. Along with variable or incremental cost, it can be a powerful pricing influence with great impact on company profit.

Here, once again, you see how important it is for managers to have a precise knowledge of the cost structure of their company and its major divisions: the fixed and variable cost components in each case. Such knowledge is essential for intelligent decisions on many pricing and related questions.

CHAPTER 13

COST OF CAPITAL: THE FUNDAMENTAL INGREDIENT

IF YOU WERE thinking about starting your own business, you would quickly recognize that your first problem is getting the capital needed for the venture. You need money to buy or lease office or plant space, to acquire necessary supplies and equipment and inventory, to employ people and meet the payroll. The same is true for all business enterprises from the smallest company to the giant corporation. The need for capital is fundamental in every case.

Once a company is in operation and has become successful, it can build capital internally through retention of earnings. The pros and cons of this practice are described in Chapter 15 on dividends. But apart from this, there are essentially only two ways in which a company can get new or additional capital. It must either add to equity participation in the company by selling stock or incur debt in some form.

When I was a young man without any knowledge of the business world, I remember being astonished to learn that a corporation could simply issue stock and people would pay for it. It struck me that this was about on a par with owning a printing press that would print United States currency. But I soon learned that this analogy was not quite correct.

While it is true enough that there are no serious restrictions on how much stock a corporation can issue, so long as buyers can be found, there is a definite penalty involved. Stockholders, in effect, own a share of the corporation in proportion to their common stock. When new stock is issued, their ownership share is diluted and its value may be reduced accordingly. You may be quite certain that corporate officers and directors will consider all this very carefully before they decide to issue new stock to obtain additional capital.

THE PROCEDURE FOR SELLING STOCK

Common stock will be issued, of course, when a company first goes public. The usual procedure is for one or more investment bankers to lead the effort by underwriting the stock. A detailed registration statement on the company is prepared, which must be cleared with the Securities and Exchange Commission and then made available, in the form of a *prospectus,* to all those interested in buying the stock. The managing underwriters form a syndicate of other investment bankers who will share the underwriting risk, and also involve other brokers, who will join in the sales effort. You can see these syndicate members listed from time to time in the financial press, with the lead underwriters at the top of the list, in what are called *tombstone* ads. The positioning of names, of zero interest to the average reader, is considered a matter of great importance by syndicate members. Indeed, some investment bankers will refuse to participate if their name is not at or near the top of the list!

The actual sale price of the stock is set at the last minute to take account of market conditions. The goal here is to set a maximum price with the key proviso that it still be low enough that the entire stock issue can be sold very quickly. If all goes well, the actual sale can then be completed in a few days. Syndicate leaders will then undertake to stabilize the stock price in the market for several weeks, and will purchase stock if necessary to accomplish this. For all their work, and taking account of the risk involved if market conditions should change and the stock could not be sold as planned, the managing underwriters are paid a significant fee. Other underwriters also receive a fee for sharing the risk and all brokers involved in the sales campaign are compensated in proportion to their actual sales.

A stock sale can be a difficult time for the officers and directors of a new company. It is a strange procedure with new and unusual hazards. Quite often, because market conditions can change drastically almost overnight, there is no certainty that the stock issue will succeed at all, and many have been canceled at the last minute for that reason. Beyond this, the transition from a private company to a public company, with all kinds of new regulations and rules to comply with, can be a traumatic experience for management. Even so, a public company has many advantages, especially in access to the capital markets, which can far outweigh all these troubles and tribulations.

In any event, this is the basic procedure required to sell securities of any kind to the public, whether it be an initial or subsequent stock offering, the sale of bonds, or the sale of any other security. Clearly the sale has to be relatively significant in size in order to make it worthwhile for a company to undertake such an effort.

THE DILUTION FACTOR

In recent years, corporations in general have met more than 70 percent of their long-term capital needs from retained earnings, with the remainder coming from external sources, either sale of stock or additional debt. The key advantage of the stock issue is that no interest has to be paid or principal repaid as with a loan, and the new capital received will strengthen the company and its net worth. The main disadvantage is the dilution factor mentioned earlier, along with the fact that dividend payments on the new common stock, unlike interest payments on debt, are not tax deductible.

Now, let's take a closer look at the dilution factor, using this example before and after the sale of additional stock:

	Initial	New	Total
Shares (000)	1,000	1,000	2,000
Earnings (000)	$1,000	$1,000	$2,000
Earnings per share	1.00	1.00	1.00

Here the company starts out with 1 million shares and sells another million. In order to avoid dilution, it must get a sufficient return on its new capital to earn an additional $1 million per annum. How difficult this may be depends, among other things, on the price obtained for the new stock. If, for example, the stock is sold for a net of $10 per share, or ten times earnings, then there would be $10 million in new capital and the company would have to earn 10 percent on this to avoid dilution. If, by contrast, the net price is $20 per share, then there would be $20 million in new capital and the company would only have to earn 5 percent on this to eliminate dilution. Any return greater than that indicated, of course, would not only avoid dilution, but add to earnings per share.

You may have noted a simple relationship here. The net price obtained for the new stock, as a ratio to current earnings per share, is the reciprocal of the yield needed on the new capital to avoid dilution. In the first case, there was a price/earnings ratio of 10, and 1/10 or 10 percent was the required yield. In the second case, there was a price/earnings ratio of 20, and 1/20 or 5 percent was the required yield. So this is a very quick way to test this aspect of a new stock issue.

This example simply proves what common sense would suggest, that the higher the price for which the new stock can be sold, the easier it is, not only to avoid dilution, but to do the opposite and increase earnings per share.

The other key factor, of course, is what the corporation expects to earn on the new capital, not only now, but in future years as well. To meet the nondilution test, per share earnings must continue to be at least equal to what they would have been without the new stock issue.

LONG-TERM DEBT

In the search for new capital, the alternative to a stock issue is some form of long-term debt. For smaller companies, the most likely source is a commercial bank. It is very important for the top executives of such companies to have an established relationship with a bank where they can deal with bank officers who know the company and its management.

If the bank considers the credit of the company to be satisfactory, it may grant a term loan of up to perhaps seven years. Such a loan may well involve collateral, or a note agreement with various restrictive covenants, or both. Personal endorsements by the owners may also be required. All this, along with the interest rate to be paid, which may be either a fixed or a floating rate, is a matter for negotiation.

Banks can lose a great deal of money in loans of this kind, when their borrowers fall upon hard times, and they naturally want all the safeguards they can get against such a loss. Thus they may be expected to maintain a lively interest in their borrowers, and their degree of financial health, until the term loan is repaid.

Larger companies have a much wider choice in sources of new capital in the form of debt. They too can turn to one or more commercial banks for a term loan, but they can also issue unsecured notes or *debentures* either in a private placement to institutions or in a public sale. Some companies may choose to sell debt securities that are secured by the company's assets, and these are called *bonds.* In a public sale, a selling syndicate is required and the overall procedure is essentially the same as in a stock issue. The company will want the debentures to carry the lowest possible interest rate, but the underwriters will want the rate to be high enough that the issue can be sold very quickly. Once again, market conditions can affect this judgment up to the day the sale actually begins.

Debentures thus issued are typically no more than promissory notes with some minimum restrictive covenants on what the company may or may not do, so as not to jeopardize its financial health until the debentures are paid off. Being long-term in nature, due perhaps twenty or thirty years in the future, debt of this kind is a fairly permanent addition to the capital structure of the issuing company.

Some debentures have a sinking-fund provision whereby a certain percentage of the issue must either be bought in and retired each year or be purchased on the open market. Because this is viewed as reducing the risk involved, it may make the debentures salable at a lower interest rate.

Debentures may also have a call provision whereby the company may call them in for redemption by paying some premium over par value. This premium typically starts high and gradually reduces as time goes on. Companies like this provision because it gives them the option, if interest rates should decline in the future, of buying in the debentures and refinancing at a lower rate. For exactly the same reason, the buyer tends to view the call provision as a disadvantage.

Typically issued in $1,000 units, debentures or bonds

that meet certain size and other requirements may trade publicly and thus be a very liquid security for the holder. The big market for these securities is with institutions such as pension funds and insurance companies and similar investors. The main attraction of debentures for corporate issuers is the interest rate, which may be the lowest available, along with fewer restrictions on the company than might be required by other forms of debt.

PRIVATE PLACEMENT

Instead of a public issue, larger companies may seek additional debt capital through what is called a *private placement*. This is a long-term loan from an institutional lender such as an insurance company or pension fund. An investment banker usually serves as an intermediary in arranging such a loan. It can be for a long period, such as 20 years, and all of its provisions are negotiable, including the interest rate and restrictive covenants.

Typically there is no collateral for loans of this type and the lenders must rely on these covenants to safeguard their investment. They will usually require that the company maintain a specified minimum of net worth, along with some restriction on dividends that can be paid, capital expenditures, stock repurchases, and so on. The company must report periodically to the lender, and if any of these covenants are violated, it is then in default and the entire loan may become due immediately at the option of the lender. In arranging such a loan, there can be a great deal of negotiating about these covenants, with the company naturally wanting to maintain as much freedom of action as possible.

A great advantage of the private placement is the flexibility that it affords. The interest rate may be either fixed or floating in relation to the prime rate or some other standard. Terms of payment may be altered to meet the needs of the borrower, including prepayment at some penalty in the form of a premium over par. In these and other ways, the loan agreement may be tailored to meet specific needs of the borrowing company. While all this is helpful to the borrower, it also has advantages for the lender. Major insurance companies and other institutions must invest large sums of money continually. As part of an investment program of this type, the private placement is not only an effective device, but one that is also fairly easy to administer.

PREFERRED STOCK

As a source of additional capital, *preferred stock* is a hybrid security, with some of the characteristics of debt as well as of common stock. Usually issued at a fixed dividend rate, preferred stock takes priority over common stock if a company goes bankrupt or is liquidated. After all the creditors are paid, preferred stock must be redeemed before any money can go to the common stockholders. Dividends on preferred stock must be paid before any dividends are paid on common stock shares, although unlike interest on debt, they are not tax deductible to the company. Like debt, however, they do add to the financial leverage of the company.

Preferred stock may also be callable, after some period of time and at some specified price. Dividends may be cumulative, which means that they continue to accrue even though the company is forced to miss one or more payments.

Utility companies and others may issue preferred stock for new capital when debt agreements or regulatory constraints make it impossible or undesirable to add any further debt to the balance sheet. Corporate investors such as insurance companies find preferred stock attractive because of a major tax deduction on its dividends. This intercorporate deduction is fair enough because the company issuing the preferred stock has already paid a full tax on its earnings before paying the dividend, and it would be most inequitable for the corporation receiving the dividend to pay the same full tax all over again.

In issuing either debt securities or preferred stock, a company may add a convertible feature whereby the security can be converted into a specified number of common stock shares in the company. From the standpoint of the investor, this adds to current income the possibility of a capital gain, and the advantage to the company may be a lower interest or dividend rate than would otherwise be required.

One other type of financing merits some mention at this point, although it is, at least in theory, short-term in nature. This is called *commercial paper* and is equivalent to a simple promissory note or promise to pay. Issued by major corporations in large denominations and sold by brokers who specialize in this market, commercial paper can be issued for any desired time period, usually 90 to 270 days, and is sold at the going interest rate at time of sale. Because of its flexibility, commercial paper is particularly well adapted to meet the seasonal needs of borrowers.

In addition, both because of this flexibility and because of the caliber of the borrowing companies, the interest rate on commercial paper tends to be quite low in comparison with other interest rates. Commercial banks, which were the traditional source for seasonal and similar loans, now find it very difficult in dealing with large customers to compete with the interest rates available in the commercial paper market.

STOCK REPURCHASE PROGRAMS

Thus far in this chapter the focus has been on ways to obtain new or additional capital. The reverse of this occurs when a company repurchases its stock and diminishes its capital and net worth accordingly. The company may have excess capital to spend for this purpose or new debt may be incurred to finance the program. In any event, it is the reverse of dilution. With a stock repurchase, the remaining stockholders own a larger share of the corporation. The question is, what is their new share worth compared with the prior share?

One quick way to answer that question is to analyze the return on investment. The company invests a given sum, perhaps many millions of dollars, in buying back its own stock. What kind of yield is it getting on that investment? Once again, the price/earnings ratio provides a quick test. If a company pays 10 times earnings for the stock, then its immediate yield on the investment is 1/10 or 10 percent. If it pays 20 times earnings, the yield is 1/20 or 5 percent. In other words, if you pay out $10 and get $1 in earnings, you have a 10 percent return. Similarly, if you pay out $20 for $1 in earnings, you have a 5 percent return.

This, of course, is a snapshot in time, and the moving picture may be quite different. Company officers and directors may consider a 10 percent return on their investment quite mediocre, and still justify buying back stock at 10 times earnings. They may reason that in a fairly short time the earnings will grow from $1 to $2 per share, in which case their earnings yield jumps to 20 percent, which most would consider a very handsome return.

There are some obvious disadvantages in any stock repurchase program. Financial strength is reduced as net worth goes down and debt ratios go up. Also lost is the opportunity to invest the same amount of money in some other way. Whatever the return on that investment might have been, it is no longer available. So there are pluses and minuses involved and the real test for the stockholder is what the net effect will be on the value of his stock over time.

The market generally looks with favor on stock repurchase programs. Although there are SEC restrictions on exactly how stock may be repurchased, so as not to affect current prices, such a program necessarily adds some strength to the demand for the stock. Beyond this, it indicates company optimism for the future, and that is always an important signal in the investment world. For all these reasons, it is not surprising that many companies have participated in stock repurchase programs and no doubt will continue to do so.

SUMMARY

When companies need new or additional capital, their essential choice is between issuing more stock or taking on long-term debt. Issuing more stock adds to the financial strength of the company, but it also reduces the ownership share of existing stockholders. The key question here is whether, over time, return on the new capital will more than offset this stock dilution.

There are several ways to obtain capital in the form of long-term debt, depending to a considerable degree on the size of the company. These have been discussed in this chapter in some detail in terms of their advantages and disadvantages to the borrower.

Preferred stock is a hybrid with mixed characteristics, partially like common stock and partially like debt. It meets a special need for some companies. Stock repurchase programs in effect take capital out of a company. They, too, have their merits and demerits, but are highly regarded by many companies and no doubt will continue to flourish.

Capital is the lifeblood of all business enterprise, and all managers can benefit from some knowledge of where it can be found and how it can be obtained.

CHAPTER 14

CORPORATE USE OF FINANCIAL LEVERAGE

RETURN ON EQUITY is a key measure of corporate and hence management performance. Return on equity, of course, is simply net income or profit divided by stockholders' equity. Because this ratio is given close attention by stockholders and security analysts, it is quite understandable that top executives of public companies take a keen interest in it as well.

For the stockholder, this ratio indicates how well the company is employing the equity capital that has been entrusted to it. Few companies pay out all of their earnings each year in dividends, and companies typically retain a significant share for company operations. So the question for the stockholder essentially is this: "Is the company return on these retained earnings superior to what I might earn from some other investment if this amount were paid out to me instead in the form of dividends?" While this is by no means all that stockholders should think about, it is certainly a very practical question that management must consider.

All this indicates why top managers of a company are likely to work very hard to increase the return on equity in their enterprise. Obvious ways to do this include increased efficiency, productivity, market share, and the like. What may not be so obvious is another way to increase return on equity through what is called *financial leverage*, which means the amount of debt used by the company as part of its capital. Those who wish to know how corporations operate in the real world should be familiar with this process and learn how it can be identified and analyzed.

There is nothing sinister about the process. Debt is commonplace in our society. Most of us participate in the debt process when we use a credit card, or buy an automobile on an installment basis, or purchase a house with the help of a mortgage. The only difference is that we typically use debt to buy things we want to consume, whereas corporations incur debt because they need the capital for growth, investment in new plant or equipment, and so on. In both cases, debt may be entirely appropriate so long as it does not strain the financial ability of the borrower.

The way a corporation can use debt to improve its return on equity is very simple. Let us consider the example of a company with $10 million in equity capital earning $1 million in net income. If this company can borrow another $10 million and invest that in such a way as to earn another $1 million in excess of interest after taxes, it will have doubled its earnings on the same equity capital, and thus its return on equity will have doubled as well from 10 to 20 percent. By this wave of a magician's wand, a mediocre ratio has been converted into a superior return on equity.

Again it must be asked, what is wrong with this? If the debt is well within the financial capability of the company, and the borrowed sum is invested for sound corporate purposes, the answer is that there may be nothing at all wrong with this strategy, and it may make good management and corporate sense.

There is, of course, a penalty for this gain in return on equity in the form of an increase in corporate risk. Interest on debt must be paid, and the principal amount of the debt must be amortized, or the company will be in real trouble. These are fixed obligations and if they are not met, the company will fall into bankruptcy. It is the same with an individual in debt. Payments must be made or else some very drastic and unpleasant things will happen.

It is this risk that management must assess when it incurs debt of any kind. Conservative management will tend to keep the ratio of debt to equity at a relatively low figure, whereas more aggressive management will be quite willing to take on a much higher ratio. Thus, when stockholders look at their company, it is important for them to consider how well their own personal attitude toward risk matches that of their company's management.

ELEMENTS OF RETURN ON EQUITY

While leverage of a company is quite important, it nevertheless is only one of the factors that enter into return on equity. Look at Table 14.1, which shows that this return—the ratio of net income or profit to stock-

TABLE 14.1

ELEMENTS OF RETURN ON EQUITY

Profit Margin	×	Asset Turnover	=	Return on Assets	×	Leverage Ratio	=	Return on Equity
$\frac{\text{Profit}}{\text{Sales}}$	×	$\frac{\text{Sales}}{\text{Assets}}$	=	$\frac{\text{Profit}}{\text{Assets}}$	×	$\frac{\text{Assets}}{\text{Equity}}$	=	$\frac{\text{Profit}}{\text{Equity}}$
$\frac{\text{Profit}}{\cancel{\text{Sales}}}$	×	$\frac{\cancel{\text{Sales}}}{\text{Assets}}$	=	$\frac{\text{Profit}}{\cancel{\text{Assets}}}$	×	$\frac{\cancel{\text{Assets}}}{\text{Equity}}$	=	$\frac{\text{Profit}}{\text{Equity}}$

holders' equity— is actually the compound result of four other ratios. In a very real sense, these ratios unravel the basic financial structure of any company and demonstrate how it operates and how it achieves its profit performance. Any manager who wants to understand how corporations work must consider all of these ratios. It is really quite simple, and the table makes all the components abundantly clear.

In Table 14.1 you see that profit margin multiplied by asset turnover equals return on assets, and return on assets multiplied by the leverage ratio equals return on equity. The box at the bottom of the table shows why this is so. When the first two ratios are multiplied, the sales figure in the denominator of the first cancels the numerator in the second, leaving profit/assets or return on assets. When this ratio is multiplied by the leverage ratio, the assets figures cancel in the same way, leaving profit/equity or return on equity.

Now to convert all this into actual figures, look at Table 14.2. Here you see actual ratios. The average figures shown are for more than 5,000 public companies, which means virtually all such companies of any size in

TABLE 14.2

ACTUAL DATA

Elements of Return on Equity

Company	Profit / Sales	×	Sales / Assets	=	Profit / Assets	×	Assets / Equity	=	Profit / Equity
Average.....	4.9%		.53		2.6%		4.85		12.6%
A	1.0		1.70		1.7		11.53		19.6
B..............	36.7		.46		16.9		1.44		24.3
C	8.3		.35		2.9		3.41		9.9
Ratio	Profit Margin	×	Asset Turnover	=	Return on Assets	×	Leverage Ratio	=	Return on Equity

NOTE: Average is for 5,332 public companies.

the United States. In the first line of data you see that the average profit margin is 4.9 percent. When this is multiplied by asset turnover of .53, the result is a 2.6 percent return on assets. And when this is multiplied by the average leverage of 4.85, the final result is a 12.6 percent return on equity.

Next, there is Company A, a grocery wholesaler picked at random, with a structure that bears little resemblance to the overall average. Here the profit margin is a sad 1.0 percent, but a relatively huge asset turnover of 1.70 transforms this into a 1.7 percent return on assets. And a truly enormous leverage ratio of 11.53 then converts this into a very respectable 19.6 percent return on equity. To turn a rather pathetic 1 percent profit margin into a near 20 percent return on equity is a very neat trick indeed. And our analysis shows precisely how it is accomplished.

Company B is a broadcasting company, in a very different industry, and the ratios here bear little resemblance to those in the preceding case. The profit margin is a very handsome 36.7 percent, and when this is multiplied by a .46 asset turnover, the result is an equally handsome 16.9 percent return on assets. When this is multiplied by the relatively low leverage ratio of only 1.44, the result is a 24.3 percent return on equity, a fine rate of return in what clearly is an efficient and conservative operation from a financial viewpoint.

Company C is really a group average for certain electric utilities. Here a profit margin of 8.3 percent, multiplied by a low .35 asset turnover, produces a 2.9 percent return on assets. And this, when multiplied by a 3.41 leverage ratio, produces a substandard 9.9 percent return on equity. No doubt this reflects the rate and similar problems of a regulated industry.

So you see here a wide range in return on equity, and an equal diversity in the factors that produce this final result in each case. The key lesson is that it can be highly misleading to base any judgment on any one of these ratios taken alone. All should be examined together to fully understand what the entire structure and the final result really mean.

You may wonder how difficult it is to get data of this kind on various companies, and the answer is that these ratios are readily available on a monthly basis in specialized financial publications, covering all public companies of any size in the United States.

SUMMARY

Return on equity is a key measure of corporate and management performance, and thus receives a good deal of attention by stockholders and security analysts. Top managers work very hard to improve this ratio in their company, and one way to accomplish this is through leverage created by taking on debt for capital that can be put to work.

There is nothing wrong with this, so long as the additional capital is used for proper corporate purposes, and the debt assumed is within the financial capability of the company. But there is always a hidden cost in that the fixed obligations of the company are increased, which is a definite risk factor. Thus the amount of leverage is always a significant clue to the management philosophy of a company (past or present) in terms of how much risk is deemed to be acceptable. Investors may or may not find this philosophy to be compatible with their own views.

But it is a mistake to think that leverage is the only device by which return on equity can be improved. On the contrary, there are three other ratios in addition to the leverage ratio that are equally vital, and all four together provide a sharp X-ray of how any company produces its final return on equity. Managers and executives who know how to compile and compare these ratios can use them as a powerful analytical tool.

CHAPTER 15

WHAT DIVIDEND PAYMENTS REALLY MEAN

SUPPOSE YOU were elected to serve as a director of your company. At the October board meeting, the president recommends that the prior quarterly dividend of 25 cents per share be continued, payable in December. What would you need to know to cast an intelligent vote on this recommendation? Assume the following facts:

Stock price	20.00
Earnings per share	2.00
Paid out in dividends	1.00
Retained	1.00
Price/earnings ratio	10.00
Payout ratio (%)	50.00
Dividend yield (%)	5.00

Here earnings per share are estimated for the current year, and dividends are shown at the annual rate. If earnings are $2.00 per share, and $1.00 is paid out in dividends, then the payout ratio is 50 percent as indicated. And a dividend rate of $1.00, with the stock price of $20.00 per share, is a dividend yield of 5 percent. Further, if $1.00 is paid in dividends, out of the $2.00 in earnings, then $1.00 is added to retained earnings of the company.

So the facts are simple enough, but what do they tell you in terms of your decision on how to vote? As a director, you represent the interests of stockholders. How can you be certain that the management recommendation is in their best interests?

You know that stockholders like income, so you might reason: Why not increase the dividend and give them more current income? What could be wrong with that? The only negative you see is that the company would then retain less of its earnings, for its own use, but does that really make any difference to stockholders?

DIVIDEND YIELD

One thing you should consider at this point is that the individual stockholders tend to think of dividends in terms of the annual dividend rate and dividend yield. Indeed, if current income is the primary goal, dividend yield may be a major factor in selecting stocks to buy, with this yield being compared with the interest rate that could be earned on some alternate savings instrument such as a certificate of deposit.

What the individual may not recognize is that dividend yield is the result of two things: the annual dividend rate and the stock price. The higher the latter, with other things being equal, the lower the dividend yield, and vice versa, as this table illustrates:

Company	A	B	C
Stock price	20.00	40.00	40.00
Earnings per share	2.00	2.00	2.00
Paid out in dividends	1.00	1.00	2.00
Retained	1.00	1.00	0.00
Price/earnings ratio	10.00	20.00	20.00
Payout ratio (%)	50.00	50.00	100.00
Dividend yield (%)	5.00	2.50	5.00

Here you see that Companies A and B are exactly alike in earnings, dividend rate, and payout ratio, but the dividend yield for Company B is only half that of Company A because of its higher stock price and price/earnings ratio. The dividend rate would have to be doubled, leaving no retained earnings, as in Company C, for the dividend yield to be the same. As obvious as this seems, it may not be entirely clear to the average stockholder.

In years past, I would get a call about once a year from a gentleman who owned about 100 shares of our stock, and he always had a bitter complaint. He would point out that he also owned some shares in a utility company with a dividend yield of about 6 percent, versus our 2 percent, and he thought it was absolutely outrageous on our part not to increase our yield to the level of the utility's. I would patiently point out that the utility stock had a very low price/earnings ratio, which made its dividend yield relatively high, and suggest that he would not be pleased if our stock price were to plunge to the level of the utility's. But he was totally unimpressed by this mathematical abstraction and would call again the following year with the same unhappy complaint.

DIVIDENDS AND STOCK PRICE

In considering the dividend question, you must also consider that stockholders should be interested not only in current income, but also in a gain in stock price over time. And it may be that a reduction in earnings retained by the company will have an adverse effect on the ultimate value of its stock. Below are some facts that bear on this question.

Of the approximately 5,300 major public companies, about one-half pay no dividends at all. Of this number, about one-half have negative earnings, and it is interesting to note that stockholders still place a value and sometimes a very considerable value on this stock, even though it is without either dividends or earnings.

Further, and perhaps the most interesting fact of all, the companies with positive earnings that pay no dividends have a higher price/earnings ratio, on the average, than companies that do pay dividends. From this you might well conclude that stockholders attach little or no importance to dividends in their valuation of a given stock.

But life is not quite this simple, and further statistical analysis indicates that among those companies that do pay dividends, there is some positive correlation between the payout ratio and price/earnings ratio. So if a company pays any dividends at all, it would appear that a higher payout ratio may have some favorable effect on the value of its stock. Be warned, however, that this is a general relationship with many exceptions to the general rule.

If you find all this confusing, you may take comfort in the knowledge that you are not alone. Indeed, it is a fair guess that many directors who vote routinely on the dividend question, quarter after quarter, are simply following a standard pattern in the company, and would find it difficult to cite any clear rationale, other than precedent, for their action.

TOTAL STOCKHOLDER RETURN

With stockholders interested both in current income and in stock price gain over time, you may now decide that the guiding principle of dividend policy should be to maximize both elements in combination in the future. Analysts call this total stockholder return, and its method of computation is shown in Table 15.1.

To work out a table such as this for any company, you must start with some hypothetical number of shares.

TABLE 15.1

TOTAL STOCKHOLDER RETURN

End of Year	Stock Price	Dividends per Share	Annual Dividends	Share Equivalent	Cumulative Shares	Total Value
0	20.00	—	—	—	10,000	200,000
1	22.00	1.10	11,000	500	10,500	231,000
2	24.00	1.20	12,600	525	11,025	264,600
3	23.00	1.30	14,333	623	11,648	267,908
4	27.00	1.40	16,307	604	12,252	330,808
5	30.00	1.50	18,378	613	12,865	385,942

Five-year increase in value 93.0%
Annual compound rate of increase 14.1%

Any number will do, but 10,000 is selected here as a nice round figure. At the end of each year, it is assumed that the annual dividends are used to purchase more shares of stock, at the year-end stock price. Then, at the end of the period, five years in this case, the value of these accumulated shares is compared with the initial value to find the annual compound rate of increase, which is the total stockholder return. This return can be calculated for any period in the past for which the data are available, or it can be calculated based on projections for future years. It can also be compared with total stockholder return calculated in similar fashion for other companies, industry groups, and so on.

If you had to select one figure to measure company efficiency, the key grade on the report card of management performance, it might well be this total return to stockholders, which includes both dividends and stock price gain, with proper weighting of each. But as vital and familiar as this measure is to stock analysts and investment advisors, it has been my experience that very few executives and managers know how it is calculated and how useful it can be in financial analysis.

OPTIMUM DIVIDEND PAYOUT

Now, if maximizing total stockholder return in the future is your goal as a director of your company, let's go back to the question of how dividend policy can contribute to this effort. What is the optimum dividend payout ratio for this purpose? How should the earnings pie be divided between dividends to stockholders and earnings retained by the company?

There is no general answer to this question, and it must be considered on a case-by-case basis, taking into account the special circumstances of the company involved. More particularly, it must focus on what the company will do with the retained earnings, and what sort of return it expects to earn on this additional capital.

Clearly, if the company has no need for additional capital, there is little justification for retaining any part of current earnings, and the dividend payout should be 100 percent. The same is true, in theory, if the expected company return on the retained earnings is less than that which stockholders might earn in other investments if all the earnings were paid out in dividends.

However, a 100 percent dividend payout is a rarity, because few companies will concede that they cannot put additional capital to work in a productive way that will materially improve their stock price and stockholder value. How can you, or any other director, make an informed decision? The problem, of course, is that you are dealing here with estimates and projections that are difficult to evaluate by any objective criteria.

PAR GROWTH RATE

There is, however, one key figure that can be quite helpful in making an evaluation: the historic record of the company's return on its own capital. This, you will recall, is the ratio of net income to stockholder equity, and what the company has accomplished here, especially in the immediate past, is at least a strong clue as to what it may continue to achieve in return on new capital.

This really is the vital hidden element in dividend policy, and if you assume that the company will continue its current return on equity in the use made of retained earnings, you can arrive at some interesting conclusions. The following data make a significant point:

	Company A	Company B
Earnings per share	2.00	2.00
Paid out in dividends	1.00	1.00
Retained	1.00	1.00
Return on equity (%)	10.00	20.00
Par growth rate (%)	5.00	10.00

Here you see a new term, *par growth rate,* which means the expected growth in earnings per share based on nothing but the return expected from retained earnings this year, assuming that the current return on equity will continue.

And you also see that although both companies are exactly the same in earnings and dividends, retention of earnings alone should produce a 10 percent increase in earnings per share for Company B versus 5 percent for Company A. This increase is entirely apart from any additional growth that can be generated from current or other operations, and it is called the par growth rate for that reason. This much growth should occur if there is no addition from other sources.

For example, if a company's growth rate is 25 percent, and its par growth rate is 10 percent, then 15 percent is due to internal and other growth excluding return on retained capital. This is a very useful thing to know, and accordingly, these data were added some years ago to the monthly *IndustriScope* publication by the Financial Services Division of Media General for all major public companies.

The calculation of the par growth rate is very simple. Take Company A, and the $1.00 in retained earnings. If the company can continue to earn 10 percent on the $1.00 thus retained, it will add 10 cents to earnings, which is five percent of the $2.00 earnings per share total. The same calculation in Company B yields a 20 cent addition to earnings, which is 10 percent of the $2.00 earnings per share.

Now, bear in mind that the stock price will tend to rise with an increase in earnings per share, and you will see that Company B has a much greater potential in this respect than Company A, even though earnings per share, retained earnings, and the payout ratio are exactly the same in each case. And this works in reverse as well, so that a higher dividend rate and proportionate reduction in retained earnings will have a greater negative impact on the earnings growth of Company B than on that of Company A.

RAISING DIVIDENDS CAN HURT STOCKHOLDERS

Two basic conclusions emerge from this analysis. First, increasing the dividend rate at the expense of retained earnings can have a definite negative impact on earnings growth and thus potential stock price gain. And second, the higher the potential return on equity in the given company, the greater this impact.

So once again you discover there is no free lunch in the financial world. Increasing dividends sounds like a good deal for stockholders, but it may come at the expense of lower earnings growth and a lower stock price in the future, and that can be very expensive. Again you see that the expected return on equity, applied to retained earnings, is the key hidden factor.

This factor sheds some light on the paradoxical fact cited earlier that companies paying no dividend, even though they have positive earnings, enjoy on the average a higher price/earnings ratio than those that do pay dividends. The former tend to be smaller and less mature companies in high-tech and other fast-growing industries. They need additional capital for growth and find it difficult to obtain it from outside sources. Thus it makes good sense for them to retain all of their earnings for growth. Their stockholders recognize this and look for their reward in terms of stock price gain in the future.

You may find it interesting to analyze your own company using the guidelines given thus far in this chapter. You are likely to find all the data you need in the latest annual report, and the results of your analysis should give you a deeper insight into your company's dividend policy.

CHANGES IN DIVIDEND RATE

As a practical matter, most mature companies have a fairly well-established dividend policy, aiming at a target payout goal of 30 percent, or 40 percent, or something of the kind, with small increases in the dividend rate once a year if earnings continue to rise. This becomes routine for stockholders and analysts and attracts little attention.

But a large adjustment in the dividend rate, especially if it is a reduction and is unexpected, can have a traumatic effect in the stock market and the stock price can tumble accordingly. A significant reduction in dividend rate, or total elimination of dividends, sends a clear message that the company is in real trouble. A substantial and unexpected increase in dividend rate, on the other hand, should have the opposite effect. Here the signal is that the company is expecting a big increase in earnings, and this should have a very positive impact on the stock price.

In brief, dividend changes, quite apart from any other significance, are interpreted in the stock market as signals of how top management and directors feel about the future of their company, and those who establish dividend policy must always give this careful consideration. If the signal is misleading, it is false advertising that can backfire.

OTHER SOURCES OF NEW CAPITAL

One of the key elements in dividend policy, as you have seen, is the company's need for additional capital in the form of retained earnings. Assuming the need exists, the question arises: Why not increase dividends and reduce retained earnings, and then get the additional capital needed from some other source such as debt or issuance of new stock?

The pros and cons of using debt as a part of capital are discussed in detail in Chapter 14 on financial leverage. Sometimes it is feasible and desirable to take on additional debt, and sometimes not.

Obtaining additional capital by selling company stock tends to be impractical on a year-by-year basis. Beyond that, it often is a very expensive way to add to capital and can dilute the holdings of existing stockholders. Retention of earnings is clearly a much easier way for a company to increase its capital.

Even so, these alternatives should be considered in any comprehensive analysis of dividend policy. In addition, there may be some restrictions on the payment of dividends. They must be paid out of earnings, either past or present, and those earnings must be available. Remember, too, that for loan security purposes, most long-term debt agreements place some kind of limit on dividend payments.

TAX IMPACT

Taxes can play a key role in dividend policy. For many years, the capital gains tax was much lower than the tax on ordinary income, especially for higher-income taxpayers. Consequently, such taxpayers would tend to prefer gains in stock price over current dividend income, while the exact opposite might be true for the lower-income individual. Thus, dividend policy could be a selective device in terms of the type of stockholder attracted to a given company.

For the moment, at least, this basic condition no longer exists because the tax differential between ordinary income and capital gains has been eliminated. It should also be noted, in this connection, that pension funds are huge investors in stocks, and are tax exempt. These fund managers, therefore, can concentrate on prospective stockholder return without bothering about tax liability of any kind.

STOCK SPLITS AND DIVIDENDS

One other type of dividend should be mentioned, and that is a *stock dividend.* In lieu of a payment in dollars, the company will issue additional shares of stock as a quarterly payment. The theory here, presumably, is that the stockholder may either keep the additional shares or sell them if there is a need for current income.

This practice, to my mind, is ridiculous. No value is created by the issuance of additional stock. Each stockholder has exactly the same share of the total pie as before. All that has happened is a lot of unnecessary bookkeeping in what is, in essence, no more than a public relations gesture.

A *stock split* is of the same basic nature. Here a company decides, for example, to distribute one share of stock (or some other number) for every share outstanding.

This is construed by the public in general and probably most individual stockholders as a wonderful thing—a true gift from heaven. In fact, it is just like the stock dividend. Once again, all the stockholders own exactly the same percentage of the company as they did before, and nothing has happened except a lot of additional bookkeeping. Other things being equal, a stock selling for $40, before a stock is split in two, should sell for $20 thereafter and stockholder value should remain the same.

The justification offered for splitting stock is that individual investors like prices in the $20-to-$30 range or thereabouts, and when the price gets higher than that, they will look elsewhere for stocks to buy. Also, it is pointed out that individual stockholders like to buy round lots of 100 shares, and a lower stock price will enable them to do this with a smaller dollar investment.

There is some merit in these arguments, and some evidence that a stock split may have the effect of increasing the number of stockholders in a given company. At the same time, large investors, such as pension funds, may find a stock split a negative factor because it increases their transaction cost when they buy or sell shares in the company. This cost is on a per-share basis, and because it takes more shares for any given dollar transaction, the total cost increases accordingly.

Many studies have been made of the impact of stock splits on stock price. Typically, where there is an increase in price, it tends to occur at or around the time the split is announced. After the split, the price may then settle down to where it was before. It is difficult to interpret the signal effect of the stock split. Often it is accompanied by an increase in the dividend payment, which is a very positive signal of company optimism about its future, and this message alone may account for any increase in price, rather than the stock split as such.

In any event, you should be aware that there is no great magic in stock splits, and no real advantage other than the possible attraction for individuals interested in buying a round lot of 100 shares for a relatively low dollar outlay. The only real significance is likely to be the message sent to the market that the company is quite optimistic about its future, and experience suggests that this message is not exempt from all the usual forecasting errors and should be construed accordingly.

SUMMARY

Anyone concerned with the dividend policy of a company should be aware of a number of considerations. First of all, it would be helpful to see the dividend record of the company for at least the last five years, showing earnings per share, dividends paid, and the payout ratio. Also useful would be a comparison with other companies in the same industry in terms of payout ratio and dividend yield.

Also relevant is an analysis of total stockholder return for the company for the prior five years, preferably in the form of the basic table presented in this chapter.

In addition, there should be an analysis of earnings per share, year by year, for the past five years, for comparison with the par growth rate as described in this chapter, along with return on equity for each of the past five years with a projection for the current year. And finally, consideration should be given to a projection of the return that can be expected on the new capital generated from the retained earnings.

With this information at hand, you are in a position to make a reasoned judgment, not only on the next dividend to be declared, but on the general dividend policy as a whole and its basic rationale, a vital element in the financial structure of any company.

CHAPTER 16

HOW TO DEAL WITH SEASONAL VARIATION

IN THE BUSINESS world, seasonal variation is a hard fact of life. The combination of calendar fluctuation and seasonal change in demand can create sharp variations in revenue and profit data. It is not unusual, for example, for some retail companies to make all of their profit for the year in the Christmas season alone.

Quite apart from seasonal factors, our rather weird calendar itself can be troublesome in the analysis of business trends. Not only do the months differ in number of days, but they also differ in that a given month may have four Sundays one year and five Sundays the next, and so on. This can have a very considerable effect, for example, on such things as newspaper advertising linage, which tends to be much heavier on Sunday and Thursday than on other days of the week.

Seasonal variation makes life difficult for business executives who are constantly trying to assess the real trend in their division or company, and whether they are moving ahead or falling back. While this may become quite evident a year or so after the fact, that is a little late for corrective action if any is needed.

So, for managers, the very real question is: How can you analyze your revenue and profit data in such a way as to tell what is really going on at a particular time? This is not an easy task, but certainly the first step in such an analysis is to try to eliminate seasonal fluctuation from the data so the underlying trend can emerge. The quick, rough and ready system in the business world is simply to compare data for a given month or some other time period with the data for the same period the year before. It is a very simple system that everyone understands, but it can be and often is quite misleading.

If, for example, a corporation reports a 15 percent increase in quarterly earnings over the prior year, the usual inference is quite favorable in terms of this year's performance. But it overlooks the fact that two periods are involved in the comparison, and it may well be that the percentage increase is more a function of poor performance last year than of good performance this year.

Similarly, reported earnings might be down, not due to poor performance this year, but rather due to superior performance in the prior year. And so it goes, with all kinds of possible combinations of the two periods, each with a very different conclusion as to this year's performance, which is unfortunate, because it is the latter that is the focus of your real interest.

There seems to be no practical way to change this procedure in the business world. It is quick and simple, and will continue to be used because there is no easy substitute for it. But all managers should be keenly aware of the deficiencies of the procedure, especially in trying to analyze their own data in terms of underlying trend. And there is a better way to do that.

SEASONAL INDEXES

Let us assume that you want to analyze the sales of your division, and that you have the sales figures each month for the past ten years. Your first step is to find for each month its percent of sales relative to the moving 12-

month total of sales in which the specified month is the center. But there are no 12 calendar months in which June, for example, is the center. In fact, it is the center of 13 months, beginning with December of the prior year and ending with December of the given year. The solution to that problem is to get the 12-month total ending in November of the given year, and the 12-month total ending in December of the given year, and then average the two.

With the 12-month moving total computed this way, and each month expressed as a percentage of its appropriate total, the next step is simply to average these percentages to get an average for January, for February, and so on. If these averages do not add to exactly 100 percent, then they should be prorated up or down until they do equal 100. The final result is a measure of how each month relates to all the other months in a typical or normal year. These figures can now be used to adjust the original data to eliminate seasonal variation.

As an illustration, suppose you are dealing with quarterly sales data of your company, and you have found from the above analysis that the average for each quarter is as follows:

Quarter	Percent of Year	Ratio to Average
1	28	1.12
2	20	.80
3	22	.88
4	30	1.20
Total	100	4.00
Average	25	1.00

The ratios to average for the different quarters are the seasonal indexes for your particular set of data.

Now, all that is necessary to adjust for seasonal variation is to divide the original data by these ratios. Thus the adjusted figure for the first quarter in any year is the actual figure divided by 1.12, with a similar division by .80 in the second quarter, and so on.

The net result of this process is shown in Table 16.1, with the actual numbers being a set of computer-generated data. The adjusted figures in the table have also been put in index form, with the average for the first four quarters (which is 988) equal to 100.

The index number has the virtue of being abstract, and thus can be compared with similar indexes computed for

TABLE 16.1

ADJUSTMENT FOR SEASONAL VARIATION

(In Thousands of Dollars)

Quarter	Seasonal Ratio	Actual Sales	Adjusted Sales	Index
1	1.12	1,132	1,011	102
2	0.80	825	1,031	104
3	0.88	879	999	101
4	1.20	1,093	911	92
5	1.12	976	871	88
6	0.80	727	909	92
7	0.88	929	1,056	107
8	1.20	1,365	1,138	115
9	1.12	1,355	1,210	122
10	0.80	1,215	1,519	154
11	0.88	1,478	1,680	170
12	1.20	2,213	1,844	187
13	1.12	2,337	2,087	211
14	0.80	1,592	1,990	201
15	0.88	1,768	2,009	203
16	1.20	2,313	1,928	195
17	1.12	2,069	1,848	187
18	0.80	1,616	2,021	205
19	0.88	1,915	2,176	220
20	1.20	2,770	2,309	234

Figure 16.1

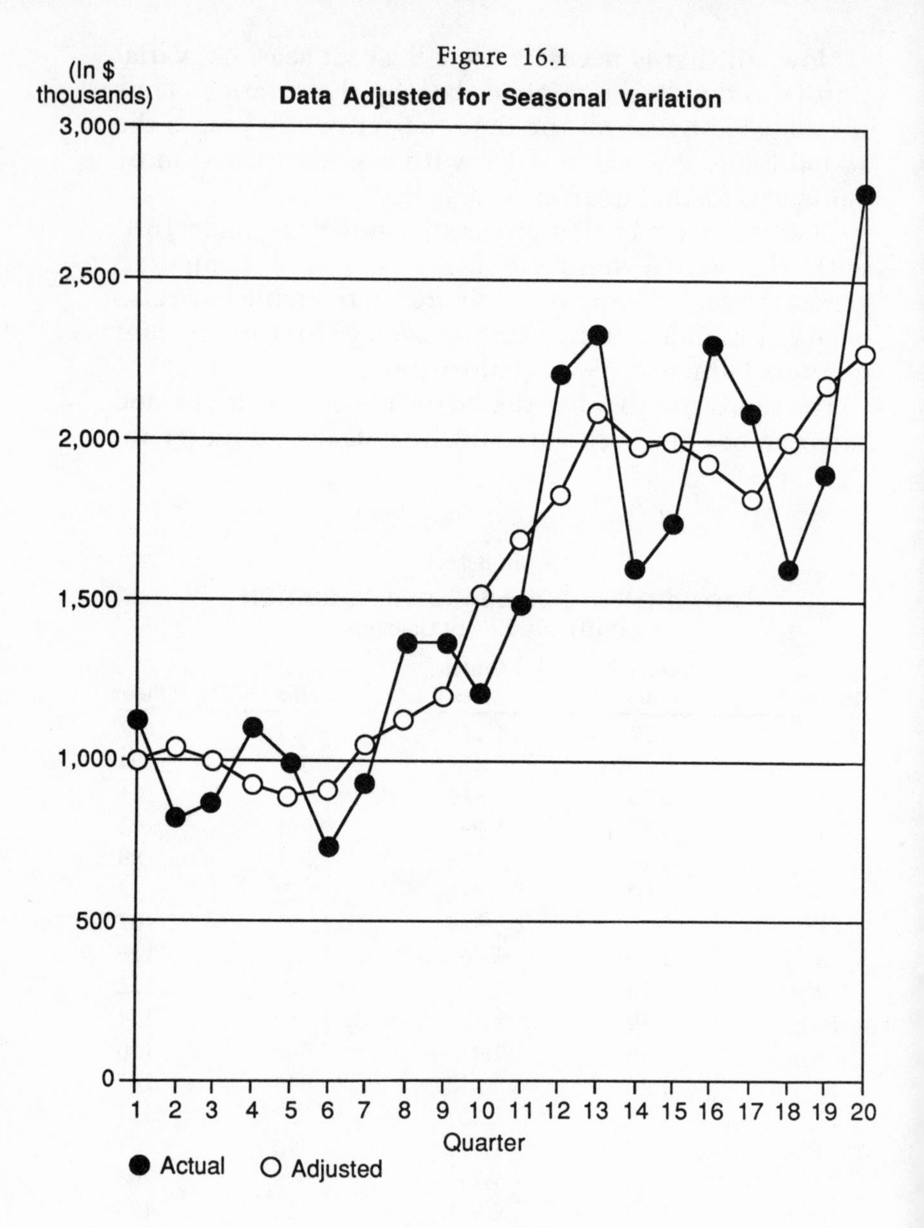
(In $
thousands)
Data Adjusted for Seasonal Variation
3,000
2,500
2,000
1,500
1,000
500
0
1
2
3
4
5
6
7
8
9
10
11
12
13
14
15
16
17
18
19
20
Quarter
Actual
Adjusted

other companies, industry groups, the gross national product, or any other time series. It is also easy to read and easy to chart. Further, it is obvious from the data in the table and even more so from the chart in Figure 16.1, that these adjusted figures provide a rather sharp picture of the underlying trend, and thus make the basic concept and reason for seasonal adjustment very clear.

Note that the great virtue of data adjusted for seasonal variation is that you are no longer confined to comparing a given period with the same period in prior years. The adjusted data for any period may be compared with that of any other period. Thus the chief executive officer of this company, looking at these adjusted figures quarter by quarter, has a realistic measure of the underlying trend. You will note, by contrast, that this is very difficult to infer from the unadjusted data.

And so, a little arithmetic and the proper technique can work some minor miracles in helping managers understand what is really going on in their own companies, and this in turn should lead to better decision-making by all concerned.

SUMMARY

Other refinements are possible in the measurement of seasonal variation. Sometimes it makes sense, before the analysis described above, to put monthly data on an average daily basis, and perhaps to adjust for the number of Sundays each month, and so on. Sometimes seasonal variation changes over time, and it is possible to make allowance for this. And still other more complex refinements are possible with the computer power now widely available.

But the important thing for the business executive is to understand the concept and the simple mechanics of the adjustment process. Once again, this is a powerful analytical tool, and a very useful thing to know.

CHAPTER 17

STOCK INDEXES CAN BE MISLEADING

INDEX NUMBERS with considerable importance in the financial world are those measuring the change in stock prices from one period to another. A number of such indexes are published regularly, with differences both in coverage, and in weighting system.

The oldest and most famous of the stock indexes is the Dow Jones Industrial Average, which dates back to 1884, and in its present form has been published continuously since 1929. It is based on 30 blue-chip companies selected to represent a broad sample of American industry. Changes are made in the list from time to time, due mainly to mergers and the like.

Originally, the average was calculated by simple arithmetic, adding all the prices per share of the included stocks and dividing by their number, and there has been no basic change in this procedure except that the divisor has been adjusted to reflect stock splits.

In precomputer days, this may have been the only practical way to compute the average in the limited time available, but the procedure is not entirely logical. To demonstrate this, let's look at two hypothetical stocks:

Stock	Price per Share I	II
A	$20	$18
B	60	66
Average	40	42

Here we see from period I to period II that the price of Stock A dropped 10 percent and the price of Stock B increased 10 percent, but the stock average went up $2 or 5 percent. The reason is that the stock price of B is three times that of A, and hence it is given three times as much weight in computing the average. This makes sense only if Stock B is three times as important as Stock A, and this is most unlikely because per-share prices are not likely to be correlated with anything other than a fondness for stock splits on the part of corporate boards.

All of which simply means that the weighting system used in the Dow Jones Industrial Average is essentially happenstance. But however deficient its rationale, this index is likely to continue in popularity for the following reasons.

In order to offset stock splits over the years, the divisor has been reduced to a very small number, and the resulting average is now in four digits, which has considerable appeal. When the Dow moves 12 points a day it sounds like something. By contrast, exactly the same change in an index with a smaller base (say a change of 1.0 on a base of 100) appears quite insignificant by comparison.

Beyond this, the index has been recorded for a very long period of time and a great deal of technical literature has been generated from it, based on various movements of the index and its cyclical behavior. And finally, the 30 companies included in the index are very large indeed and thus represent a significant share of the total valuation of all stocks on the New York Stock Exchange. So it would be expected that the stock price of these companies would reflect broad movements in the market, however crude the averaging method used.

But sophisticated analysts look elsewhere for a more accurate measure of stock prices, and generally turn to the S&P 500 Index. Published by Standard & Poors, this index includes 500 of the largest companies in the nation, with representation in all key industries. The S&P 400 is a component of the total, restricted to industrial companies only.

Price indexes are computed by weighting individual prices by some appropriate quantity. In a consumer price index, for example, prices are multiplied by the quantity of each item consumed in a typical family budget. For stock prices, the obvious quantity is the number of shares outstanding for each stock. When this is multiplied by price per share, the result is total market value, which may then be added, for various stocks, to create an aggregate price index. This is the procedure used for the S&P indexes, and for a number of other stock indexes as well.

So what is being measured, in effect, is the change in total market valuation of the stocks included in the index. This is a useful concept, and no one can fault its logic, but it should be recognized that larger capitalization companies will tend to dominate such an index. Because of this dominance, such an index may not be a good measure of what is happening to stock prices in general.

With this in mind, it was decided many years ago that the Media General Financial Services Division should create a new stock index that would be more representative of what was happening to the average stock, and this index has been published continuously since that time in the Media General Financial Weekly.

In constructing this index, a theoretical $1,000 was invested in each stock in the base period, and the index measures the total value of this portfolio ever since. All stocks on both major exchanges and the larger OTC (over-the-counter) stocks are included in the index. The net effect, of course, is to give equal weight to each stock. A 10 percent change in the stock of a small company is just as important as the same change in the stock of a large company. Thus the index is a good measure of what is happening to stocks in general at any given point.

As might be expected, this index can differ sharply from others that are dominated by companies of large capitalization, and has often outperformed the latter by a significant margin. There may be some lesson in this for the average investor, who can achieve a high degree of diversification by investing approximately the same amount in each of 20 or 30 stocks representing a variety of industry groups. Such a portfolio will tend to track the market as a whole, with a limited potential for loss in any given stock. If the stocks are selected on a rational basis, such a portfolio over time may well outperform others put together in a less balanced format.

SUMMARY

Although the Dow Jones and S&P indexes have clear limitations in representing stock price changes in the market as a whole, they continue to be the basic yardsticks used by portfolio managers to measure their own relative performance. These and other indexes are quite necessary in measuring the change over time in stock prices. They can be constructed in a variety of ways, and results can differ accordingly. For executives interested in the relative performance of pension and similar funds, it is useful to know how the various indexes are put together and what they mean.

CHAPTER 18

HOW TO READ AN ANNUAL REPORT

COMPANIES SPEND large sums to make their annual reports as attractive and interesting as possible. Yet it is very likely that few stockholders or executives know how to read these reports and take full advantage of the information they contain.

If you are a stockholder or potential stockholder, or an executive in a given company, or considering a job in still another, you should pay careful attention to the annual report of the company involved. This is perhaps your best opportunity to learn how top management feels about the company in terms of its current position, immediate outlook, priorities, and objectives.

For purposes of this chapter, I have selected an annual report at random from the many that cross my desk every year. The name of the company is not significant for the discussion here, and thus it will be called Company X. First impressions are important in terms of readability, and this report comes out with high marks in this respect with a clean, elegant front cover, featuring a colorful photograph of a family in a recreational environment. Incidentally, you can find some of the finest examples of commercial printing and photography in annual reports, both in design and in quality of reproduction. Outstanding creative people work on these projects and the results reflect their high degree of expertise.

You may wonder why companies go to all this trouble and expense. In some degree, of course, it is simply a matter of corporate pride. But beyond that, most good managers feel a keen sense of responsibility to their shareholders, who own the company, and are quite serious about their duty to report on how well that responsibility has been discharged. Even though stockholders themselves may not read the report as carefully as they should, these managers know that security analysts—who follow the company in terms of investment potential—are certain to read it very thoroughly indeed, down to the last footnote.

There are some exceptions. Occasionally you will find a company whose management will put little more in its annual report than the bare minimum that is legally required. Various reasons are cited for this unusual approach. Sometimes a company is so big and well-known that management sees no real need to explain and describe it to shareholders. In other cases, management simply takes the viewpoint that the key numbers speak for themselves, so why waste money on an expensive annual report. All of which proves that companies can and do differ rather sharply in personality.

The cover of the Company X annual report is certainly attractive. Now, let's turn the pages and see what we find. Inside the front cover there is a brief profile of the company describing its three major business segments and the division of its revenues between the United States and overseas markets. Also listed here is the table of contents for the report.

On the opposite page are the financial highlights for the year just concluded. Most managers tend to believe that this is the best-read section in the entire annual report and, indeed, that it may be the only section that most people read. As a result, most companies tend to pack a great deal of information in their financial highlights page, and this is true of Company X. For each item reported, there is a total for the year being reported on and the prior year, with the percentage change shown in each case.

The first item listed is net sales—well over $10 billion—so it is clear that our random choice is a very large company indeed. Sales are also up 14 percent over the prior year, which is substantial growth. Next appears pretax income at more than $500 million and net income of more than $300 million, with the latter up 22 percent, a significant gain. This is followed by net income per share, of special interest to stockholders and also up 20 percent over the year before, along with the number of shares outstanding.

In the succeeding block of data, working capital is listed at nearly $300 million, capital expenditures at about $450 million, depreciation at about $200 million, long-term debt at about $900 million, and stockholders' equity at about $1.6 billion. Then dividends and book value per common share, and return on stockholders' equity of 21.4 percent, which is a superior return.

At the bottom of this page are two simple but powerful charts that show the sales and net income of the company for the past 10 years. During this period, you can see that sales were up every year but one and net income was up every year over the prior year. Further, the trend is not only up in both cases, but curving upward, which means an increasing amount of growth each year.

These two charts and the brief financial data tell quite a story. From what you have learned in other chapters in this book, you can draw a great many inferences about the strength and viability of this company from the simple facts reported on this one page alone.

LETTER TO STOCKHOLDERS

Next in this report and in most others is the direct communication to stockholders by the top executive officers of the company. Here is their opportunity to comment on performance during the year, problems and achievements, current outlook and plans for the future. You may be quite certain that top executives give a good deal of thought to this message, and that every word in it is chosen with great care.

First of all, they know that this message must be as accurate and truthful as they can make it, because any attempt to deceive can have some very bad consequences for all concerned, including both civil and criminal penalties. Indeed, you must bear these constraints in mind as you read any letter to stockholders. Put yourself in the place of these top managers, and you can see why most of them tend to be quite conservative in their comments, especially in anything that might be construed as a forecast. They are fully aware of the uncertainties in any such forecast and wary of making promises that may not be kept.

Beyond this, some chief executive officers may not be disposed to say much more than they have to in their annual report, and the letter to stockholders may be restricted to no more than a brief mention of key performance figures. And this alone tells you a good deal about the management of a particular company.

Any company of reasonable size is likely to have some problems during the year, and it is always interesting to see how they are treated in the letter to stockholders. They are unpleasant for management to talk about, but when they are discussed with full candor, confidence in company leadership goes up accordingly.

In brief, therefore, you should pay close attention to the letter to stockholders in any annual report. Learn to read between the lines and you can learn a great deal about the company from what is said and what is left unsaid. Both can speak volumes to those who know how to interpret this specialized and formal communique.

In the Company X report, the letter to stockholders takes two pages and includes a photograph of the top executives. It is a very straightforward statement. It points to the 20 percent growth over the prior year in earnings per share and the 21 percent return on equity, two important factors for stockholders to consider.

The letter goes on to say that the increase in sales has been driven primarily by unit volume, rather than price increases. It briefly mentions a divestiture and an acquisition. Then there is a statement that it is the company's mission to be the leading brand-name food and consumer packaged foods company, and this is spelled out in four separate criteria.

The letter then says that the goal of management is to maintain real growth in earnings per share (inflation adjusted) of at least 8 percent per annum, which is superior to any publicly stated goal of any competitive company. Along with this, management also hopes to achieve at least a 20 percent return on equity. Finally, it is said that prospects for the coming year are pleasing, and it is hoped that the solid growth of recent years will continue.

All of this constitutes an unusually strong and courageous statement by top management, clearly expressed in very simple terms, and should be most reassuring to stockholders of the company.

REMAINDER OF ANNUAL REPORT

The next two pages of the Company X report are devoted to a brief analysis of annual operations and listing of officer and director changes, along with a bit more detail on acquisitions and divestiture, corporate mission and strategies. The report then turns to financial performance and reports total stockholder return over the past 10 years compared with the S&P 500 Index and return on United States Treasury bills. At 24 percent per annum for the past 10 years, stockholder return in the company has far exceeded the other two comparative indexes.

The report then analyzes the trend in long-term debt versus stockholders' equity, and states that it is company policy to keep such debt within 35 percent of total invested capital. It further states that the company has been able to maintain high credit ratings on both its long-term debt and commercial paper.

Following this is a discussion of financial leverage, the ratio of total assets to equity, and how this has improved return on equity for each of the past five years. It is unusual to see this spelled out so clearly in an annual report, and the discussion is quite helpful in explaining the company's performance in recent years.

OTHER INFORMATION

The report continues with a discussion of the company's major brands and summary data on their performance, a very colorful and informative section. It is followed by the formal accounting report, balance sheet, and net income statement, duly certified by an outside auditor. From what you have learned in earlier chapters in this book, you will know that this is a gold mine of useful data.

Finally, there is a listing of the board of directors and key officers, and a final page devoted to useful investor information on such things as time and place of the annual meeting, dividend payment dates, dividend reinvestment program, and so on.

In conclusion, I think this report is very nearly a model for what an annual report should be. It is thorough and yet brief, unusually clear and straightforward. By any standard, it must be considered a first-rate communication to stockholders, investors, and employees.

SUMMARY

If you know how to read an annual report, it can tell you a great deal about any company, but you need to know what to look for and how to interpret the material. Many if not most of the analytical techniques described in this book can be applied to the information provided in any company's annual report. The result can be a sharp insight into its financial strength and operating structure.

At a minimum, all managers and executives should be thoroughly familiar with their own annual reports, and preferably those of their principal competitors as well, and thus take full advantage of this valuable resource.

CHAPTER 19

ADJUSTING FOR INFLATION

YOU WILL RECALL the key point made in Chapter 4 that dollars coming due at different dates in the future are not equal in value. In order to be comparable, they must be adjusted to a common standard: their present value equivalent.

Similarly, dollars in past years are not equal in purchasing power because of inflation. To achieve comparability, any monetary series in the past must be adjusted to eliminate the inflation factor. This is quite easy to do but, in my experience, many managers are not familiar with the simple arithmetic involved, and thus are a little uneasy in their interpretation of the final adjusted figures. Here is the simple procedure required.

Suppose you are interested in a specific three-year period and have selected an appropriate price index as follows:

Year	Price Index	19x1 = 100	Dollar Value
19x1	113.6	100.0	100.0
19x2	119.8	105.5	94.8
19x3	131.7	115.9	86.2

The price index has some prior period as a base, which equals 100, and normally you would want to convert this so that the first year in your analysis is the base. All you need do, year by year, is divide the price index by the 113.6 value for the first year and express the result as a percentage, with the result shown in the third column above. From this you can quickly see that the price level in the second year was 5.5 percent greater than the base, and in the third year, 15.9 percent greater.

What does this translate into in terms of purchasing power of the dollar? Put the third column in ratio form (move the decimal two points to the left), and divide it into 1, and the answer appears in the fourth column. Here you see that the value of the dollar, based on this price index, dropped from 100 cents in the first year to 94.8 cents in the second year and 86.2 cents in the third.

In mathematical terms, the fourth column is a reciprocal of the third column. They are the mirror image of each other in the sense that when they are put in ratio form and multiplied together, they always equal 1. Thus, to remove the effect of inflation, you can either divide by the price index or multiply by the dollar value equivalent. In practice, it is simpler to divide by the price index, but this illustration may help to clarify the concept involved.

MEASURING REAL INCOME

Now, suppose you want to analyze a given salary to see what has happened to it in terms of purchasing power. Based on the same price index, the results are as follows:

Year	Price Index 19x1 = 100	Salary in Current Dollars	Salary in 19x1 Dollars
19x1	100.0	30,000	30,000
19x2	105.5	35,000	33,175
19x3	115.9	37,000	31,924

The "Constant-Dollar" Dow

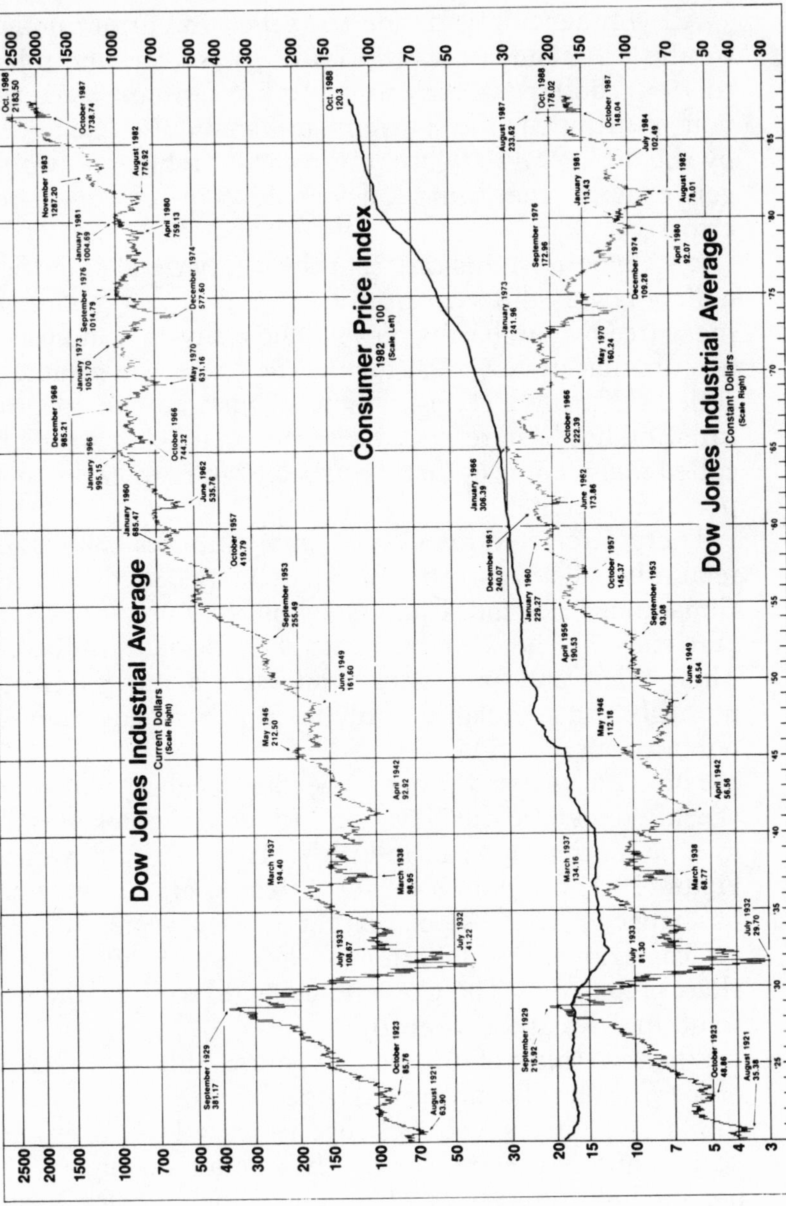

Dow Jones Industrial Average
Current Dollars
(Scale Right)

September 1929 381.17
October 1923 85.76
August 1921 63.90
July 1933 108.67
July 1932 41.22
March 1937 194.40
March 1938 98.95
April 1942 92.92
May 1946 212.50
June 1949 161.60
September 1953 255.49
October 1957 419.79
January 1960 685.47
June 1962 535.76
January 1966 995.15
October 1966 744.32
December 1968 985.21
May 1970 631.16
January 1973 1051.70
December 1974 577.60
September 1976 1014.79
April 1980 759.13
January 1981 1004.69
August 1982 776.92
November 1983 1287.20
October 1987 1738.74
Oct. 1988 2183.50

Consumer Price Index
1982 100
(Scale Left)

Oct. 1988 120.3

Dow Jones Industrial Average
Constant Dollars
(Scale Right)

September 1929 215.92
October 1923 48.86
August 1921 35.38
July 1933 81.30
July 1932 29.70
March 1937 134.16
March 1938 68.77
April 1942 56.56
May 1946 112.18
June 1949 66.54
September 1953 93.08
April 1956 190.53
October 1957 145.37
January 1960 229.27
December 1961 240.07
June 1962 173.86
January 1966 306.39
October 1966 222.39
May 1970 160.24
January 1973 241.96
December 1974 109.28
September 1976 172.96
April 1980 92.07
January 1981 113.43
August 1982 78.01
July 1984 102.49
August 1987 233.62
October 1987 148.04
Oct. 1988 178.02

Left scale: 2500, 2000, 1500, 1000, 700, 500, 400, 300, 200, 150, 100, 70, 50, 30, 20, 15, 10, 7, 5, 4, 3

Right scale: 2500, 2000, 1500, 1000, 700, 500, 400, 300, 200, 150, 100, 70, 50, 30, 200, 150, 100, 70, 50, 40, 30

Years: '25, '30, '35, '40, '45, '50, '55, '60, '65, '70, '75, '80, '85

Source: Media General Financial Weekly

All you need do is divide the salary in current dollars by the price index (in ratio form) to convert the salary to 19×1 dollars as shown in the last column. Again, if you multiplied the current dollar figure each year by the dollar value figure in the earlier table, you would get exactly the same answer (except for rounding errors).

It is obvious in this case that the salary trend in current dollars is very different from the trend in real income as measured by purchasing power. The analysis, simple as it is, puts that in very clear focus. The process in general is called *deflating* a series, which means that the effect of inflation has been removed, and the final result would be called *real* income as distinguished from current dollar or nominal income.

There are a number of price indexes published regularly. Perhaps the most widely used is the Consumer Price Index published by the Bureau of Labor Statistics of the United States Department of Labor. This index and its major components are published monthly and are readily available in various government publications.

The CPI is used by the Media General Financial Weekly to deflate the Dow Jones Industrial stock average in a chart that appears monthly. The result, shown in Figure 19.1, presents a rather different picture of what has happened to the stock market over the years. Another typical example of deflation is shown in Figure 19.2, a chart prepared by The Conference Board to show the real trend in sales and inventories.

When we think of inflation, of course, it is not in terms of the price level at any given time, but rather in terms of the rate of inflation: the change in price level from one year to another. Here, again, The Conference Board has prepared an interesting chart on changing price levels covering the period not too long ago when the inflation rate in this country soared well into the two-digit range. This is shown in Figure 19.3.

Figure 19.2

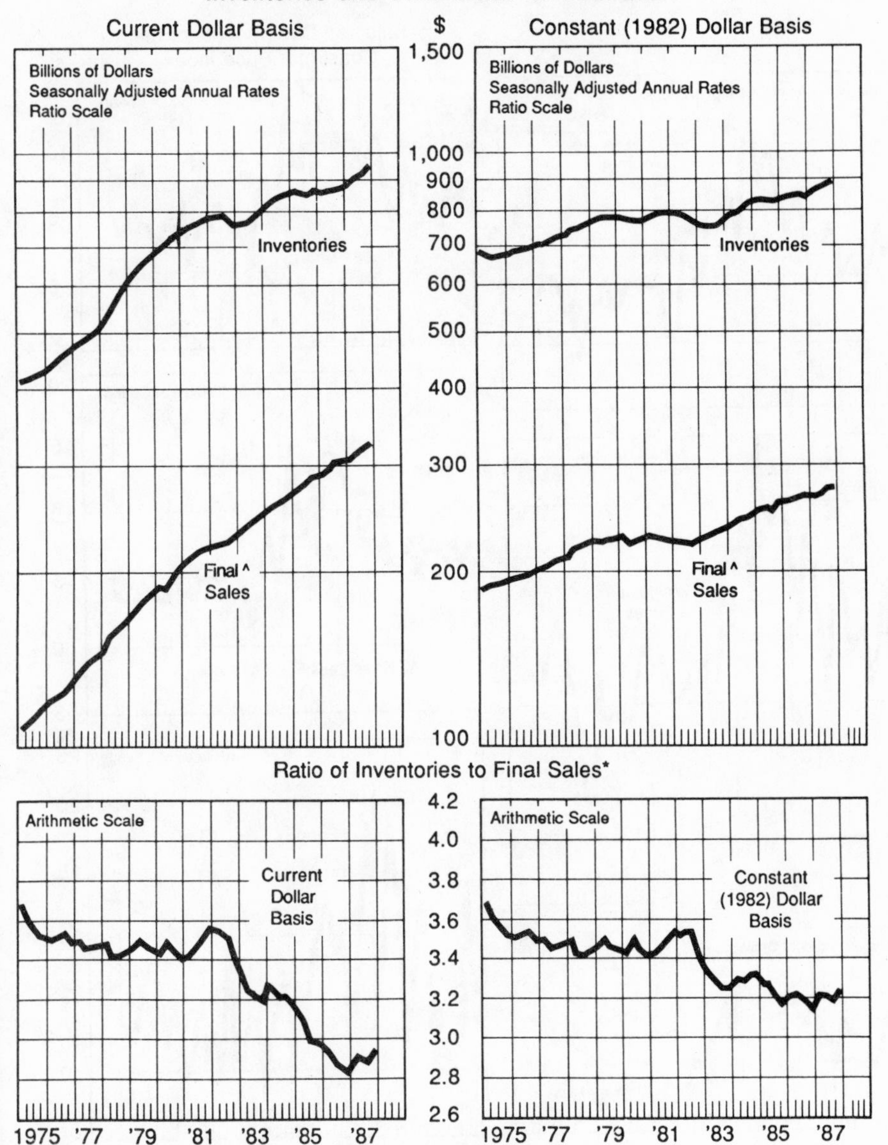

^Quarterly totals of monthly rates.
*Ratios show number of months of inventories available at current sales rate
Sources: United States Department of Commerce; The Conference Board.

Figure 19.3

Selected Price Indexes

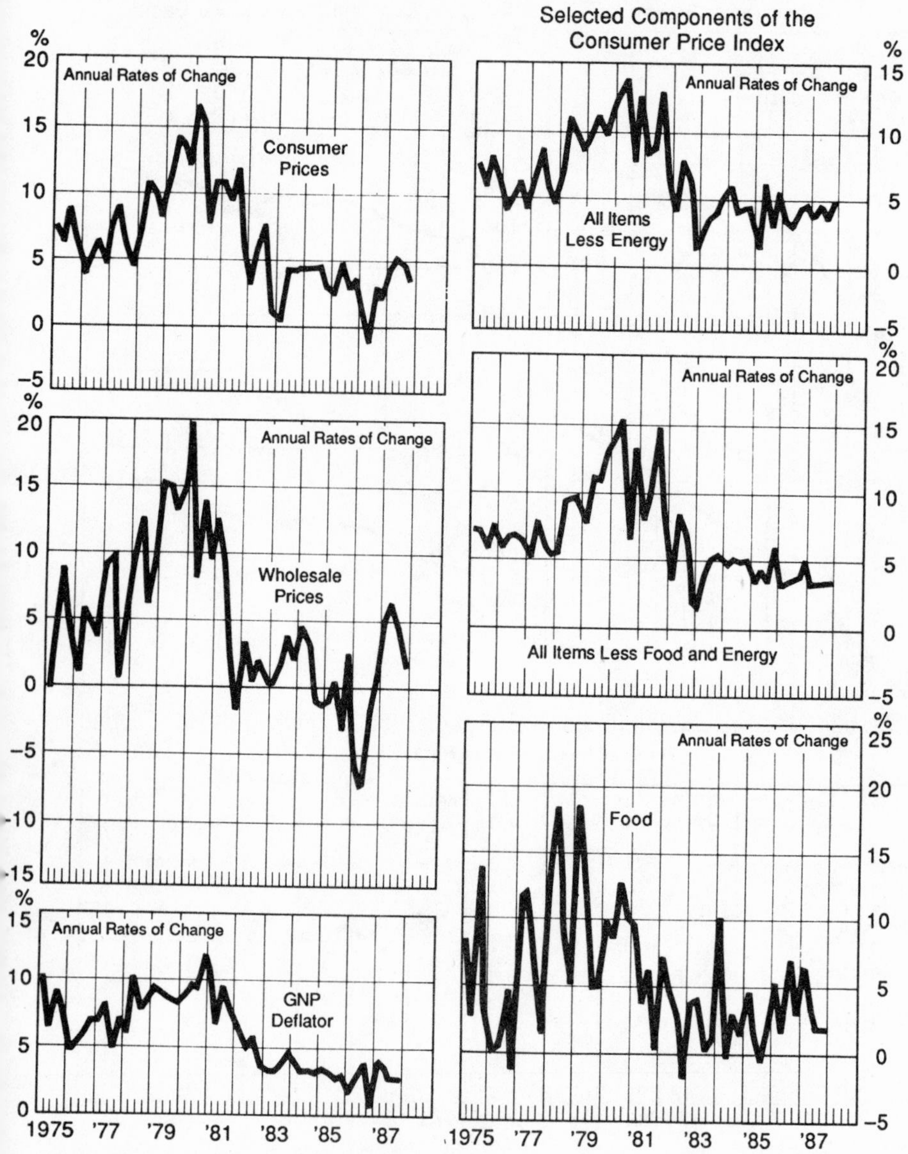

Sources: United States Department of Labor; United States Department of Commerce; The Conference Board.

SUMMARY

Inflation is a deadly blight on the economy of many countries today. It also distorts almost every historical time series of data. The only way to overcome this is to deflate the series with an appropriate price index by the simple mechanism explained in this chapter. Managers would do well to understand this technique, which has wide application in the business world, and to make use of it in their own analysis and interpretation of data.

CHAPTER 20

HOSTILE TAKEOVERS AND MOUNTAINS OF DEBT

PUT YOURSELF in the position of the chief executive officer of your own company. You pick up your newspaper at breakfast one morning, and discover that your company has been selected as the target of a hostile takeover. Or maybe the notice comes by way of a letter, or a brief telephone call late Friday afternoon. In whatever form, this thunderbolt out of the blue comes as very bad news indeed. Your company may have taken years to develop and grow to its present status, with the help of a large corps of dedicated employees and executives. All this counts for precisely nothing when the corporate raider appears on the scene.

Hostile takeovers are now a commonplace, and it is a rare day when one or more major companies are not struggling to mount some defense to an onslaught of this kind. There was a time when only small or medium-size companies were subject to takeover, but that is no longer true. Now it is not unusual for one multibillion-dollar corporation to find itself under attack by some other corporation of similar or larger size. This massive destructive force is reshaping corporate balance sheets and exerting a profound influence on decisions made in boardrooms throughout America.

A takeover attempt may come in various forms. It may be one corporation trying to take over another for purposes of growth or diversification. Or it may be one or more individuals who see in a hostile raid the chance to make a fast profit at minimum risk. Or it may be the top executives in the target company itself, who see a potential for great personal wealth in buying out the public stockholders and taking the company private in what is called a leveraged buyout.

While the type of raider may vary, there is a good deal of similarity in the impact on the target company. At the worst, the company may be dismantled, its assets and divisions ripped apart and sold. At best, traumatic changes may be made in the target company in both personnel and operations. And in almost every case, a huge amount of debt is incurred to finance the takeover. Very often, there is marginal ability to amortize this mountain of debt, which could lead to dramatic failures and bankruptcies in time of recession. All this clearly has serious implications, not just for the target company and its personnel and customer base, but also for the national economy as a whole.

METHOD OF ATTACK

To consider how a takeover attempt is conducted, let's take the case of one or more individuals who decide to launch the effort. Their method of attack is quite simple. The raiders, usually with the help of a major investment banker and working through some corporation they control, pick a company they consider vulnerable and quietly begin buying stock in the company. After a point, as a legal requirement, they must report their stockholdings and specify their intent, and their effort is then out in the open for all to see.

Typically, the next step is either the commencement of a tender offer for at least a majority of the company's shares or a merger offer submitted to the board of directors of the target company. When either offer is announced, arbitrageurs who specialize in takeover activities are likely to start buying company stock and, in aggregate, may quickly accumulate a substantial number of shares.

If, for example, company stock is selling for $40 per share and the offer is $50 per share, and the arbitrageur believes the offer will succeed within a reasonable period of time at either $50 or a higher price, then clearly there is a major profit potential in buying the stock at its current price or at a still higher price if it is less than the $50 offer.

What this means, if the directors approve a vote by the stockholders, is that the stock accumulated by the takeover individuals plus that held by arbitrageurs is often quite sufficient, no matter how the other stockholders vote, to approve the merger offer and the company, in effect, will be sold to the new owners.

All this may happen very quickly, so that company management and its directors can find themselves, without any real warning, in the midst of a legal storm of hurricane force. If they want to defend the company against the corporate raider, they must turn immediately to lawyers and investment bankers who specialize in this field, and prepare to engage in all-out corporate warfare.

THE ROLE OF DIRECTORS

Directors are in a particularly difficult situation because they must balance the short-term profit for stockholders if the offer is accepted against the possibly greater long-term value for stockholders if the company remains independent. If the raider's offer is rejected, they will almost certainly be sued for negligence or bad judgment and failure to properly discharge their responsibility to stockholders. There are law firms that specialize in such suits. They find a stockholder with a few shares and then file a complaint in his name. They hope the suit will qualify as a class action for all stockholders, whereupon their legal fees, often for a nominal amount of work, can be enormous. Even if the suit is wholly without merit, it still has great nuisance value in terms of time delay in our case-loaded court system, so that huge fees are sometimes paid to these lawyers simply to drop the suit.

The corporate raider has a great advantage in this bitter warfare in that very little capital is required, relative to the size of the target, to launch the takeover attack. Much of the money needed to buy the initial stock in the target company may be borrowed, with very little actual equity required. Then, through sources such as commercial banks or investment bankers or other institutions, standby credit can be obtained for the money needed to complete the takeover. Once the takeover is completed, the raider can use the assets of the company itself to refinance or pay off this debt.

Thus companies especially vulnerable to the corporate raider are those with valuable assets and resources that can be stripped away and sold piecemeal, including separate subsidiaries and divisions of the company that can be sold as independent operations. Any company of this type is vulnerable if its breakup value is greater than its current stock price. Needless to say, this description fits many of the finest corporations in the nation.

RAIDER MOTIVATION

The individual raider has no hesitancy in making his own motivation crystal clear. Profit is the name of the game. He holds himself out as a great benefactor of all the stockholders. He will see to it that they can sell their stock for a substantial premium over the current price. Any profit for him is simply a justifiable reward for making all these good things happen. There is no consideration of the net impact on company employees, executives, customers, suppliers, and communities where the company is involved. All this is basically irrelevant to the raider in the hot pursuit of fast profit.

It is a ruthless, cold-blooded game, and the corporate raider can be certain that many will support his effort. Institutional money managers for pension funds and the like, with heavy investment in common stocks, are trained to think in terms of profit on their portfolios and tend to look with favor on anyone who promises to contribute to that goal. If forced to choose between short-term gain and future value, they are under heavy pressure to select the former. In general, there is little doubt that many on Wall Street like the takeover game because it provides excitement and a constant stimulus to the market. Speculation about possible takeover candidates can build investor enthusiasm and generate broker sales.

Once a company is put in play by a raider, the directors may decide that their only course of action is to find a more suitable buyer, a white knight, who may be willing to pay a higher price, and a search of this kind may be launched. At the same time, others may be induced to get into the bidding contest with a higher offer of their own. Again, all this tends to happen at lightning speed, with everyone under extreme pressure. And once again, directors are fully aware that no matter what they do, they are likely to be sued. Whatever happens, the target is not likely to operate for very long as a separate, independent company.

LEVERAGED BUYOUT

Another type of takeover occurs when top executives of a company, working with an investment banker or some investor group, put together a merger plan to acquire the company with some combination of cash and debentures, and then convert it into a private company. This is called a *leveraged buyout* or an *LBO* because most of the purchase price tends to be in the form of debt. Debentures offered to investors or stockholders are usually subordinated to other debt, with little or no real collateral, and thus are called junk bonds. They typically pay a high interest rate, although the actual payment may be deferred for several years. Other key executives may also be given the opportunity to buy stock at a low price to add to their motivation to remain with the new private company and make it succeed.

An LBO takes on many aspects of any other hostile raid. If it succeeds, the aftermath may be much the same as a raider takeover. Drastic steps will likely be required to reduce the heavy debt, including sale of company assets and divisions. Replacement of machinery and equipment will be held to a bare minimum, along with a ruthless slashing of all expenses, in order to maximize cash flow.

Investors and executives who participate in an LBO usually plan to reduce the debt materially and then, in five years or so, take the company public again and sell their stock at a huge profit. It is a risky endeavor but, if it succeeds, the rewards to those who participate can be very substantial.

THE ARITHMETIC OF AN LBO

To understand the arithmetic of an LBO, let's take a very simplified example of a company earning $10 million a year after taxes, with 5 million shares of stock outstanding and a current stock price of $20 per share, or 10 times earnings, all of which is fairly typical. The top executives of the company, based on its income statement and balance sheet, consult with an investment banker and decide they can afford to buy out the public stockholders for $30 per share, a 50 percent premium over the current stock price, and then take the company private. How can they do this?

The answer appears in Table 20.1. The *Before* column of numbers shows the company before the buyout. The *After* column shows its financial status thereafter. Where

TABLE 20.1

LEVERAGED BUYOUT ARITHMETIC

(In Thousands Except Stock Price)

Item	Before	After
Stock Price	20	30
Shares	5,000	5,000
Market Value	100,000	
Debt	0	150,000
Revenue	500,000	500,000
Cost	480,000	500,000
Wages and salaries	300,000	300,000
Other operating costs	170,000	170,000
Depreciation	10,000	10,000
Interest	0	20,000
Operating Profit	20,000	0
Income taxes	10,000	0
Net Income	10,000	0
Dividends	5,000	0
Retained earnings	5,000	0
Net Cash Flow	15,000	10,000

there was no debt before, there is now $150 million in debt, used to support the buyout. While there was no interest before, there is now $20 million annual interest on this debt.

The assumption in this table is that there is no change in wages, salaries, or other operating costs. Yet the company is able to pay this extra $20 million in interest and still end up with a net cash flow (from depreciation charges) of $10 million per annum that can be used to retire debt. Indeed, the net cash flow is only $5 million less than it was before the buyout ($10 million in depreciation charges plus $5 million in retained earnings.)

It is obvious from the table where the savings are achieved. The new interest charges have wiped out the operating profit of the company, thus eliminating the $10 million previously paid in income taxes. And, of course, the $5 million in dividends to stockholders is gone as well. The main financial advantage of the LBO, therefore, comes in the substitution of debt for equity and the ability to deduct interest on the debt from taxes.

In practice, needless to say, things are not likely to be as neat and tidy as they are in this simple table, but it does make clear the basic mechanism involved in a leveraged buyout and why it can be highly attractive to its various participants.

DEFENSES AGAINST TAKEOVERS

There is a sharp division of opinion today on whether hostile takeovers serve a useful purpose. Those in support of them maintain that they are needed to shake up or get rid of lethargic management for the benefit of all stockholders. They believe takeovers also contribute to improved efficiency, which benefits the entire economy.

Others take strong issue with this position. In their view, hostile takeovers are a major disruptive influence on corporations in general and the nation as a whole. They see any short-term gain to stockholders as a minor offset to the destructive force unleashed on companies and their employees and communities. They are concerned about the mountains of debt being created and the ability of the issuers to service the debt if hard times should come.

There is no clear-cut national policy on takeovers. Congress is divided on the basic issue and there are mixed rules and regulations by the bureaucracy. Sentiment against hostile takeovers may be strongest at state level, and a good deal of state legislation has been enacted to help corporations build a legal defense against the corporate raider.

You may have heard, for example, of the poison pill defense. Here the company issues warrants to all of its stockholders. If the company is merged into a corporation controlled by the raider, the warrants will enable company stockholders to buy stock of the raider's corporation at a substantial discount from market value. Even if a corporate raider merely purchases 10 or 20 percent of the company's stock, stockholders other than the raider can then use these warrants to purchase additional shares from the company at a substantial discount from the current market price. The net effect, of course, is to dilute dramatically the value of the raider's stock in the company.

Also as a deterrent to the raider, some companies have entered into very generous long-term contracts with a number of their executives, often providing for substantial severance pay, that become effective with a hostile takeover. These are the "golden parachutes" that you read about, condemned by many but justified by corporations as necessary protection for key executives who might otherwise feel compelled to seek other employment as soon as the raider appears.

Still other legal defenses include staggered terms for directors, which make it impossible for the raider to get immediate control of the board. Also, a company's charter may require that a supermajority of the directors or the stockholders, such as 80 percent, must vote in favor of a merger before it can be approved. A similar percentage for approval may also be required of stock owned by stockholders other than the raider. And so it goes as companies search for some protection from the modern-day pirates of the corporate world.

In any event, while there is much policy discussion at all levels of government, the takeover game goes on and it is easy enough to identify the main losers when a given company is acquired and ripped apart.

It is also easy to see who wins. In many ways, the cards are stacked in favor of the raider. The capital investment of the individual raider tends to be quite small in relation to the profit potential if the merger effort succeeds. And even if his own offer fails, he has a good chance of selling his original stock in the company at a profit, either to another, higher bidder that may acquire the company or sometimes to the company itself in a transaction called "greenmail."

Thus the corporate raider is likely to be a winner no matter what happens. Other winners are the investment bankers involved, whether acting for the buyer or for the target company, and the lawyers on both sides who specialize in this type of activity. In each case, the fees tend to be quite substantial—if not astronomical—by normal standards. In a recent dramatic illustration, a relatively small but elite law firm representing a takeover candidate charged, for two weeks' work, a fee of $20 million. Even the other practitioners in this specialized and lucrative field were impressed by this performance.

SUMMARY

Hostile takeovers are a current fact of life in corporate America. Companies most vulnerable are those with a relatively low stock price. They are doubly vulnerable if their stock price is less than their liquidation or breakup value and they have assets or divisions that can easily be stripped away and converted into cash.

This vulnerability is well understood by top executives and directors and puts them under strong pressure to sacrifice future growth potential in favor of short-term gains to bolster the stock price of their company. While there is no way to quantify this, it clearly is a profound influence in executive offices and boardrooms throughout the nation.

There is little that any individual manager or executive can do about any of this except to understand the phenomenon and how it can affect the policy decisions of any company.

CHAPTER 21

MERGERS AND ACQUISITIONS: FINANCIAL STRATEGY

A FRIENDLY MERGER or acquisition is outwardly quite different from a hostile takeover, but if you are an executive with the company being acquired, you may find little difference between the two in terms of your own personal situation. Either way, it can be a traumatic and threatening experience for the individual executive.

You may wonder what is behind this kind of corporate activity, the trading of companies back and forth, which is so common today. Much of it may be due to an increasingly popular management theory that a corporation should view its various subsidiaries and divisions as a portfolio of investments. Under this theory, corporations should dispose of operating units with a low return on equity and poor growth prospects, while investing new capital in operating units with high return and promising potential.

It is a cold doctrine, but many managers find it hard to argue with its logic. From a stockholder's viewpoint, it makes little sense to keep pumping capital and management time into marginal operations when these vital elements could be better used for more promising ventures. In any event, the lesson for the individual manager or executive is pretty clear. If you have a choice, try to tie your career to an operating unit that looks attractive under the portfolio theory.

There are, of course, other reasons why corporations decide to sell or buy companies. Sometimes the acquiring corporation is looking for growth, or sees a special synergy with the company being acquired, or wants a greater market share, or is seeking diversification. There are many such reasons, often quite valid from a strategic viewpoint.

An interesting case was recently reported in the *Wall Street Journal.* Here are the first few paragraphs in the lead story:

> LONDON—Grand Metropolitan PLC just two years ago was itself a candidate for a takeover and breakup. It made dog food. It brewed beer. It ran hotels. What it didn't have was a focus—or a reputation for management.
>
> But 1986 is ancient history. Meet the new Grand Met. Last week, it sold its prestigious Inter-Continental hotel chain, leaving behind—with no regrets and a fat capital gain—the business in which it started out 31 years ago. This week, it turned around and sprang a $5.23 billion tender offer on Pillsbury Co., the bedraggled Minneapolis food and restaurant company.
>
> Grand Met now is poised to join the ranks of the world's biggest consumer goods makers. With Pillsbury, Grand Met's annual sales would soar to about $15 billion, rivaling powerhouses like Philip Morris Cos. in the U.S. and Nestle S.A. in Switzerland. At the same time, Grand Met would get the chance to show all the world its new-found increasingly well-regarded marketing prowess.

Here we have an example of the modern acquisition theory at work in its most dramatic form, combining a friendly sale of a subsidiary with a forced-takeover attempt on another company, all in multibillion-dollar figures. These few paragraphs also make fairly clear the basic rationale behind these two major moves.

NORMAL ACQUISITIONS

Normal acquisitions, of course, are much more modest than this spectacular example, and it may be useful to look into some of the procedures and mechanics involved.

First of all, companies looking for acquisitions will soon get on the list of investment bankers and business brokers who specialize in arranging corporate marriages. Their fee is normally but not always paid by the seller, tends to be a standardized rate based on the value of the transaction, and usually is quite substantial.

These brokers refer to companies being sold as *properties,* and they continually search for possible sellers. In addition, of course, if the broker is well known in a particular field, a potential seller may initiate the contact. Once the broker and seller have reached agreement on fee and related matters, including acceptable potential buyers, the broker typically will prepare a brochure on the property being sold, including a narrative description, along with its current balance sheet and income data for a number of years past, with perhaps some projection of the future.

With this material in hand, the broker will get in touch with potential buyers. If they express any interest at all, he will then send them the brochure with the understanding that it will be held in strict confidence. This is quite reasonable, of course, because there clearly are many reasons why the seller would not want it generally known that the property was up for sale.

Now, if a potential buyer shows any real interest, the broker will arrange a meeting with the seller, and may have little or nothing to do with the transaction from that point on. It is now up to the buyer and seller to reach agreement, if they can.

The main question that must be resolved, as you might imagine, is the price to be paid for the property. There are never any absolute guidelines on what a company is worth, but both buyer and seller usually have a pretty clear focus on what they think the value is, and start their negotiations on that basis. If the company being sold is a public company, then of course there is a market price for its stock, and this is a logical value to consider. But the seller usually has a variety of reasons why this price is grossly inadequate and why a substantial premium is justified.

Another logical criterion is the earnings impact of the acquisition on the acquiring company. If the acquisition will add $1 million per year to earnings, for example, and the acquiring company's stock is selling for 10 times earnings, then $10 million will look like a fair price to the buyer. But again, all this is subject to negotiation, and the final result may well deviate materially from objective standards such as these.

STRUCTURING THE ACQUISITION

A related question is how the property will be bought. Will the buyer pay cash, or perhaps some combination of cash and debt, or use stock issued by the acquiring company? From an accounting standpoint, will the transaction be structured as a *purchase* or as a stock-for-stock merger in what is called a *pooling of interests?* The decision on this is complicated by tax implications with varying impact on the buyer and the seller.

If, for example, the transaction is structured as a purchase and the buyer acquires all the stock or assets of the company being sold, current tax law and accounting principles permit a revaluation of all the tangible assets, often to a much higher level than their book value on the balance sheet.

To see why this may be advantageous, let's take the following example: A company buys all the assets of a radio station for $5 million cash. The net worth or book value of the station is only $2 million, but after its acquisition, the buyer has an independent appraisal made that raises the current value of the tangible assets to $5 million. If later approved by the IRS, this larger sum can be depreciated accordingly for tax purposes over a period of years, so the true cost of the station is not $5 million, but rather that sum less the taxes that can be deducted on the new appraised value. If the acquiring company is paying a corporate income tax of about 50 percent, the net effect is to cut the true price of the station in half. Tax laws change and all this is approximate, but the key point is clear.

This feature of our tax law explains why buyers are sometimes willing to pay what appears to be a very high price for certain acquisitions, far out of proportion to the earning power of the company being acquired. The only disadvantage in this approach is that the increase in annual depreciation charges must be deducted from reported income. But when individuals or private companies are the acquirers, they typically care nothing about this because they have no real interest in earnings reported on their private financial statement. Their interest is focused entirely on cash flow and they are delighted with tax savings from the higher depreciation charges.

TAX-FREE MERGER

The seller is in a different situation. In most transactions that would qualify for purchase accounting treatment, he must pay an immediate tax on the capital gain involved. Thus, he might prefer a *tax-free merger* of his property into the acquiring company, which requires among other things that stock in the acquiring company be exchanged for at least a majority of stock, or substantially all the assets, of the company being acquired. In this case, the seller pays no tax at all on the sale, until the stock received is itself sold at some later date.

The significance of this, from the standpoint of the buyer, is that no write-up of assets is permitted. In the radio station purchase, for example, with its major stepped-up basis after acquisition, there would be a substantial loss in future tax benefits.

But it is a very different story if the assets cannot be written up by any significant amount. In that event, the buyer purchasing the station would be required to account for the difference between the $5 million paid for the station and its net worth of $2 million by putting $3 million in *goodwill* on its balance sheet. This goodwill must be depreciated over a period of years, and thus will detract from earnings, with no tax benefit whatsoever.

The only way for the buyer to avoid this unhappy situation is through a merger that qualifies from an accounting standpoint as a pooling of interests. This requires, among other things, that at least 90 percent of the stock of the acquired company be exchanged for stock of the acquirer. When this occurs, the balance sheets of the two companies are simply merged, and no goodwill is involved.

In all of this, of course, the IRS plays a very active role. It must approve any write-up of assets and typically will require very strong evidence to support it. And whatever method of purchase is chosen, you can bet on one thing. If one side of the transaction gets a tax advantage of any kind, it is just about a certainty that the IRS will see to it that a comparable tax is levied on the other side. The agency takes a very dim view of any deviation from that principle.

COMPLETING THE TRANSACTION

Once the matter of price is resolved and the structure of payment is determined, the transaction is well on its way to completion. Questions remaining tend to be legal in nature, and typically are the subject of a good deal of discussion by the lawyers on both sides. Sometimes, sad to say, such discussions can reach the point of total absurdity, with an incredible amount of haggling over some minor detail. Here, as in many other contract negotiations, there is no doubt that countless potential agreements have been blown skyhigh by the senseless behavior of an overzealous lawyer.

At some point—the precise timing will depend upon the significance of the acquisition, the relative certainty that it will be completed, and the presence of rumors in the market—public companies are required to issue a release explaining that some tentative agreement has been reached or, at least, that negotiations are under way. Once this is done, the buyer can usually extend his investigation by visits to the company to be acquired for interviews with its key executives, full discussion with its auditors, and so on. Then, if all goes well, after a period of time for all the legal work to be finished, the acquisition is completed.

There are, of course, many variations on the procedure just described. Some corporations have intensive programs for development with a capable staff to oversee this activity. They may conduct elaborate research to identify proper areas for expansion, and specific companies therein that meet their acquisition criteria, followed by aggressive action to accomplish this goal.

Some private companies or subsidiaries of public companies have been sold by *sealed bid.* In this process, for example, an investment banker may select a very limited number of qualified buyers and provide those who indicate any interest with a descriptive brochure on the company being sold. Sealed bids are then required by a certain date, and the buyer may choose among them. This approach may be quite effective when there are a limited number of acquisition prospects in the field, a small number of qualified buyers that can easily be identified, and when the company being sold, such as a newspaper company, has a strong franchise position in its market.

AFTER THE ACQUISITION

What happens after acquisition depends on its purpose and the management philosophy of the acquiring company. If the new parent corporation believes in strong central control, then the new subsidiary may quickly be stripped of all staff functions and reduced to a purely line operation. At the other end of the spectrum, if the parent corporation believes in decentralization, the acquired company may be left to operate very much like an autonomous, independent unit.

All this, of course, is highly significant for the individual manager or executive in the acquired company. Jobs and careers are clearly at risk in the process of absorption by the parent company, even though the initial intention may have been to make no change in the executive staff. Realistically, as time goes on, executives in the acquired company must prove their value to the top managers of the parent.

Perhaps the best advice to anyone caught in this situation is to adapt as quickly as possible to the new circumstances. Every corporation has its own culture and philosophy and way of doing things. The manager or executive in an acquired company may find it very difficult to accept these changes and make the transition, but it is vital to do so if he wants to continue as an effective member of the management team. Avoid the error of concluding that the changes brought about by the acquisition are all negative. The positive side is that these changes may create new potential for career growth. It is always useful to bear in mind the basic reason for the acquisition in the first place.

REASONS FOR ACQUISITION

As indicated earlier, there are many reasons why a corporation will make an acquisition. A strong reason, in many cases, is simply a desire to grow. Well-managed growth, in and of itself, is a goal of most companies. It is widely believed that corporations either move forward or slip backward, and the latter is an unattractive alternative for stockholders as well as management and employees.

Beyond this, there are some clear advantages in pure size as such. The larger company is likely to have greater access to credit and the capital markets, at lower cost and on more favorable terms, than the smaller company. It has more resources for research and development and experimentation. It can attract and afford to pay highly skilled executives for vital line and staff operations. All of this can be most advantageous.

In addition, there can be significant gains in efficiency due to economies of scale. If, for example, a retail chain were to acquire another retail chain and thereby double in size, clearly there should be many management and overhead costs that would not double, thus increasing overall efficiency.

Diversification is another reason for acquisitions. Companies may seek diversification for the same reason that investors tend to choose a variety of stocks in different fields for their portfolio: to spread the risk. Clear examples can be found in R. J. Reynolds and Philip Morris, which have made significant acquisitions in food and related industries.

But diversification can be carried to excess if acquisitions are made helter skelter with no common thread and no real rationale for the hybrid combination thus created. This is the pattern of the conglomerate, which captured the interest of Wall Street for a time, but is no longer regarded with much favor. A conglomerate operates on the theory that managers are instantly interchangeable and can quickly switch from one line of business to another without any loss in effectiveness. On the basis of a fair amount of experience, this theory is now viewed as highly suspect.

Another form of diversification is to acquire companies that differ in cyclical behavior, in an attempt to cancel the impact of the national business cycle. The acquiring company may be quite prosperous on the up cycle but hard hit when business turns down, and may look for an acquisition that will be the opposite. If this can be accomplished, it may be a very sound strategy.

Some companies are interested in acquisitions for purposes of integration. A good example can be found in major newspaper chains, most of which have some ownership of newsprint mills. With newsprint being their major raw material, these companies view such ownership as a guarantee of their source of supply as well as insurance against inflation and future price increases.

Sometimes an acquisition is simply the cheapest way to get control of essential assets and production facilities. Natural resource companies, for example, often have a market value that is far less than the replacement cost of their tangible assets and equipment. For a newspaper chain, it may be much cheaper to buy a newsprint company than to build its equivalent in a new mill.

In summary, there are many reasons why an acquisition may or may not make good sense from a strategic viewpoint. Top managers of the acquiring company will normally be quite sensitive to these reasons, and to what they hope will be a favorable reaction on the part of stockholders, stock analysts, and the investment world in general. In addition, they know that other criteria will be closely examined as well.

ACQUISITION CRITERIA

One of the first things that stock analysts want to know about an acquisition is whether there will be any dilution of earnings in the acquiring company. This is easy enough to calculate. Very simply, it is what earnings per share will be after the acquisition compared to what they would have been without it. If earnings per share would have been $2.00 without the acquisition, and drop to $1.80 with the acquisition, there has been a 10 percent dilution.

Normally, you would expect the price of a company's stock to vary with earnings per share, so news of this dilution might very well cause the stock price to drop, which stockholders do not like. So dilution is a bad word in the investment world, and top managers of a company will try to avoid it whenever possible.

But there may be mitigating circumstances. Sometimes the dilution is for one or two years only, and from then on the acquisition is expected to produce a very helpful boost in earnings per share. In this case, the temporary sacrifice may be viewed as negligible in relation to the ultimate gain. Or it may be, for a variety of reasons, that overall advantages to be gained in other ways from the acquisition far outweigh the dilution cost. In any case, the investment world will want an explanation.

In some circumstances, there may be the opposite of dilution: an acquisition may add to instead of subtract from the earnings per share of the acquiring company. Consider this example. Company A is acquired by Company B through an exchange of stock, based on a pooling of interests, for a sales price equal to 15 times its own earnings. The acquiring company's stock has a market price equal to 30 times earnings per share. Consequently, there must be an increase in the earnings per share of Company B because, on a proportionate basis, more total earnings are added than new shares of stock are distributed to complete the acquisition.

This is a clear illustration of how a company can benefit in acquisition economics when its stock is highly rated by the market in terms of its price/earnings ratio, with a strong competitive advantage over other potential buyers with stock less favorably rated. This was essentially the technique used by Gannett over a period of many years to acquire small private newspaper companies all over the United States on the way to achieving its remarkable growth record.

Another financial test that can be applied to an acquisition, and perhaps the most significant of all, is the expected return on investment. Here the projected cash flow from the acquisition over a period of years, perhaps 10 or more, is related to the cost of the acquisition. You will recall that the method for calculating return on investment was described in Chapter 5, and the result is a single figure, the internal rate of return, that represents the annual compound rate of return. This calculation can provide a definitive answer because most companies will have fairly precise standards of what is acceptable, such as a return of no less than 15 percent. The process is subject to all the usual forecasting errors, but in concept it is a sound and comprehensive approach to the evaluation of any investment.

It is obvious that complex financial elements enter into any final decision on an acquisition. Dilution is a factor, but it must be weighed against intangible values and must be considered, not just for the present, but also for future years. Further, even though dilution may be negative for a time, the expected rate of return on the acquisition may be most attractive over a period of years. All of these factors merit very careful consideration.

SUMMARY

There are many reasons why corporations get involved in mergers and acquisitions. Desire for growth is a major factor, because growth can bring many benefits. Sometimes acquisition strategy is aimed at diversification, to spread the risk and moderate the overall impact of business cycles. At other times there is a need to integrate production and supply facilities. Some acquisitions are designed to increase economies of scale, or to attain greater dominance in market share. Thus, an acquisition can be a sound strategy that will strengthen the acquiring company and add to its efficiency.

On the other hand, there are bad acquisitions that serve no useful purpose from an overall strategic viewpoint. And even when acquisitions are strategically sound, they can turn out to be disappointing for a great number of reasons that could not be anticipated. External growth can be a fine thing for a corporation, but top managers soon discover that it carries with it a great deal of inherent risk.

Company executives and managers should be aware of both the advantages and the disadvantages of an acquisition. If your company is the one acquired, it can have a profound effect on its structure and operations—and your career. If yours is the acquiring company, careful preparation and planning are required, as well as knowledge of the probable consequences.

CHAPTER 22

FINANCIAL FRAMEWORKS FOR COMPENSATION SYSTEMS

IF YOU HAVE ever worked on a departmental budget, you have a clear grasp of how important compensation expense is in total operating cost. Wages, salaries, and employee benefits not only represent a major item of expense, in a magnitude that tends to swamp other components on a financial statement, including operating profit, but typically they are the dominant cost elements over which management has direct control. As a result, in comparing two competitive companies, total compensation per unit or dollar of sales is a key measure of operating efficiency.

Thus it is appropriate to consider how companies develop their systems of compensation and the underlying rationale in each case. As an executive or manager, you may have particular interest in methods of compensation and how your company policy compares with others.

To begin with, let us consider the executive bonus and some of the various forms it may take. Most companies of any size now have some kind of executive bonus and, indeed, may have several varieties in effect at the same time depending on the level of the individual in the overall executive structure. The theoretical goal, of course, is to motivate the executive with an incentive that is designed to maximize performance on the company's behalf, and the key question is how to set up a bonus system that will accomplish that objective.

Typically, the higher the individual in the executive structure, the larger the bonus relative to salary. This makes good sense on the theory that the impact of the executive on overall company performance tends to rise with his position as measured by salary, along with the fact that the higher-paid individual is perhaps better able to cope with the uncertainty of the bonus component of total compensation.

At the chief executive officer level, for example, it is fairly common to find bonus payments equal to one-half of salary or thereabouts and, in exceptional cases, equal to or greater than salary. The latter is likely to occur in companies with sharp cyclical fluctuation in profit, where the bonus for the chief executive officer is based on total earnings of the company.

These exceptional bonus payments are likely to receive a good deal of publicity and generate cries of outrage, sometimes by stockholders, but perhaps more often by union officials who are looking for ammunition to use at the bargaining table. Such payments may actually be minor, when related to company profit or the total payroll of the company, but this perspective is rarely given and thus some bonus figures do seem altogether outrageous to the average wage earner, and no doubt to the general public as well.

In some cases, it may be that these large bonus payments are not justified, but in my judgment such cases are in the minority. Decisions of any chief executive officer can have a profound effect on a company and its future profits, and total compensation paid to such an officer is usually a negligible fraction of this potential profit impact.

What the chief executive officer can do to help or hurt the company and its potential depends, of course, on the type of company and the industry in which it operates. There is an obvious difference, for example, between a mature public utility and a new electronics company in terms of the relative contribution of any executive officer. Executive bonus systems should obviously be designed to reflect these differences: the larger the potential, the greater should be the relative reward. In some companies the chief executive officer is truly vital to the well-being of the organization. Without this one individual, the company might literally cease to exist, and maximum incentive for such an individual clearly makes good corporate sense.

The competitive job market is also a key factor. First-class top executives are a rare group and in considerable demand. Any company paying less than the going rate for such individuals is in danger of losing its valuable executive talent, very costly and difficult to replace.

These considerations apply in one degree or another to all managers and executives. Bonus payments should reflect their performance in terms of company welfare, with consideration also being given to compensation levels in the competitive job market. This brings us back to the practical question of how to design a bonus system that will accomplish these goals.

THE EXECUTIVE BONUS SYSTEM

Early in my executive career, I was placed in charge of several departments in the company I worked for, and I soon learned that there was a major problem in the cooperation or, more specifically, the lack of cooperation among these departments. It was a rare day when there was not some complaint from at least one department head about some act of negligence or incompetence in one of the other departments.

It was not a new situation. It had existed for many years and was the normal environment in which everyone worked. It was not that the department heads disliked one another, but simply that their goals and objectives differed. The head of production cared only about production and the head of sales cared only about sales, and neither had any real concern for the problems of the other. I persuaded the key executives to have regular meetings to coordinate their work. But while that was useful, the net result was far short of what I had hoped to achieve.

It was in this context that I hit upon the idea of an executive bonus system for all the department heads and their main assistants, sufficient in magnitude to represent a real incentive, which would be keyed directly to the profit earned by the company as a whole. It was a revolutionary concept for our company at that time, but after a good deal of high-level discussion, the plan was approved.

The result exceeded my fondest hopes. There was an almost instantaneous change in attitude among the top executives, and it quickly trickled down to all personnel. All of a sudden, the other department ceased to be the enemy and became instead a stalwart friend and ally in the common cause. And the net improvement in overall efficiency was truly astounding.

Where all else had failed miserably, this simple bonus system succeeded to a remarkable degree. And really for a very good reason. Talk about the need for cooperation is just talk. But when everyone benefits personally and directly from cooperation, the virtue of that approach becomes very tangible, real, and persuasive.

In a sense, the bonus system had made all these key executives partners in the enterprise, with the same motivation as owners of the company, and that is very different from the motivation of an executive concerned only about the operation of his own department and how that might affect his weekly or monthly paycheck.

So we were thoroughly sold on this bonus system and, as time went on, applied the same concept to various subsidiary operations as our company continued to grow, with the bonus for the executives involved in each case keyed to the profit earned by their own subsidiary. Based on this experience over a long period of time, I believe that it is a highly efficient system and would allow many companies to build high morale along with improved performance.

OPERATING A PARTNERSHIP SYSTEM

There is, in my view, a right and a wrong way to set up the mechanics of an executive bonus system of this kind. The wrong way is to establish a bonus pool as some percentage of company profit and then divide the pool among those who participate in it, with each participant receiving some fixed percentage of the total each year. The difficulty with this procedure is that it causes major problems whenever a change occurs in the number of executives who participate in the pool, whether current participants leave or new executives are added. In either case, the percentage assigned to each executive must be adjusted so that all percentages still add to 100, and this is in conflict with the basic concept that the bonus for each executive should vary in direct proportion to company profit.

It is easy enough to overcome this by assigning to each executive, not a percentage of a pool, but rather a bonus base related to some specified year, with the actual bonus paid each year bearing the same ratio to the bonus base as profit in the given year bears to profit in the base year.

For example, if a given executive is assigned a bonus base of $20,000 related to year one, and in year three the company profit has grown 20 percent over year one, then the bonus earned by the executive that year is $20,000 plus 20 percent, or $24,000. And so the process continues in future years, unless the bonus base is changed.

It is a very simple and flexible system. New executives

can be brought into the plan with an appropriate bonus base, and others can leave, without affecting any other executives in the plan. It is equally easy to recognize increased responsibility and promotion for any executive by a proper increase in his bonus base at any time.

So these are the simple mechanics for setting up a bonus plan that has the effect of making every executive participant a true partner in the total enterprise, with all the benefits that accrue from that type of participation and motivation. In my view, the salary for each individual should be entirely adequate as total compensation, so that the bonus becomes a true plus. If that is not true, and the salary is basically inadequate without the bonus, then it seems to me that the real purpose of a bonus system is defeated.

In such a bonus system, the executive, as a partner of the enterprise, must expect his bonus to rise and fall with the fortunes of the company. One of my senior associates, many years ago, argued vehemently against this concept on the grounds that executives made greater effort in bad years than in good, and should be rewarded accordingly, and not be made to suffer in compensation as well.

There is some equity in that belief, but you cannot have these two things at the same time. To reward the executive for greater effort is not the same as making him a partner in the enterprise. In the first case, he is being treated as an employee; in the second as an owner. In my experience, most executives will unhesitatingly choose the latter position, notwithstanding the occasional hardship. They are quite willing to accept the bad years if they know they will benefit accordingly when the good years come.

One great virtue of the partnership bonus system is that the amount of the bonus is determined on a completely objective basis by the amount of company profit in a given year, as distinguished from other systems in which some evaluation by superiors can affect the total amount to be paid. While the bonus base for any executive can be changed at any time (with proper notice to the individual), once this base is established it automatically fixes the bonus amount each year.

Again, on the basis of long experience, I think most executives much prefer this kind of system. And, once more, the reason is very simple. Where superiors must decide what the bonus will be, the executive is being treated as an employee instead of as a partner, and thus much of the necessary motivation disappears.

EXCEPTIONS TO THE RULE

Admittedly, such a bonus system may not work for all companies because of special circumstances of one kind or another. And, in very large companies, it may not make sense for managers and executives down the line to whom total corporate profit is little more than an abstraction. In the latter case, however, keying the bonus to subsidiary or division profit may be a sound alternative.

It is a mistake, however, to install any bonus system, no matter how sound in concept, on a purely mechanical basis without careful consideration of all the factors involved. Every company at every point of time is a special situation and should be considered as such. For example, a profit-sharing concept may not be very sensible for a cyclical company in which the profit is heavily dependent on external circumstances over which company executives have no control. In this context, setting a profit goal at the beginning of the year and fixing the bonus of each executive in relation to that goal may be the only practical course to follow.

Where a company has a very large number of executives, and it is virtually impossible to determine how any one executive can influence even a small segment or division of the company, the profit-sharing concept loses much if not all of its significance. As an illustration of this, I served for many years on the board of a regional bank that grew to the point where it had more than 1,000 officers. For an organization of this size, a much more precise and rigorous compensation system that can be applied uniformly throughout is almost mandatory.

There are national firms that specialize in the development and application of bonus and compensation systems. They evaluate each managerial or executive job and give it a numerical rating that fixes the salary range for that position in relation to the competitive job market. Once this is done, a range is also established for the percentage of salary that can be paid as the annual bonus, with the actual percentage to be determined by some evaluation of the executive's performance during the year.

The great virtue of this type of system is the ease with which it can be administered in a company with a large number of executives. Such a system is easily explainable and almost runs itself, on a purely mechanical basis, all of which has great appeal for human resource managers and for top executives who must oversee the entire process. It also has clear advantages for the individual executive in terms of fairness and objectivity in setting overall compensation levels.

It is important to note here that these compensation systems are designed to rate jobs, not individuals. Each job is given a salary range, and the performance of the individual can be recognized by where his salary is fixed within the range, along with the percentage of salary paid out in the annual bonus. If there is a problem with the system, it is likely to be found in the evaluation of individual performance, which is necessarily a subjective process, by one or more of the supervisors involved.

There is no way in any compensation system to eliminate all elements of subjective judgment, but every well-managed company will try to be certain that every precaution is taken to eliminate bias and unfairness in the process. And a special word of caution is in order when individual performance ratings are coupled with a management-by-objective plan.

Plans of this type are often viewed as very attractive by top management. In theory, at least, it sounds like a good idea for an executive to sit down with the supervisor once a year and agree on objectives to be accomplished in the next twelve months. The problem, in this fast-moving world, is that priorities can change rather quickly, and what seemed important at the beginning of the year might turn out to be relatively unimportant as the year goes on. But if the executive knows that he will get a performance rating based on the original plan, there is likely to be considerable reluctance to make any change in priorities, however sensible that may be.

In theory, this difficulty can be overcome if there are meetings throughout the year to reevaluate priorities. But in my experience, no one much likes these meetings, neither the executive nor the supervisor, with the result that no reevaluations are likely to be made. For this reason, I am very dubious about coupling an individual performance rating, for either bonus or salary purposes, with any management-by-objective plan.

Another concern has to do with the impact on the executive involved. To illustrate this, suppose Mary Smith was rated superior by her supervisor last year, and excellent this year, with the result that her bonus drops from 15 to 12 percent of her salary. In actual dollars, the difference may be very little, but its psychological effect may be great. For a few dollars' difference, a fine executive is made to feel inferior, which is the exact opposite of the positive motivation that a good bonus system is supposed to provide. Formal bonus systems of this type are no doubt quite essential for large companies, but great care must be taken to avoid the pitfall of mechanical application, with a result quite contrary to that which is intended. In all fairness, however, personnel consultants who devise these systems understand this problem, and do their best to warn and guard against it.

OTHER FORMS OF EXECUTIVE COMPENSATION

Of all the many forms of executive compensation, annual salary itself, of course, is the most basic. Many elements enter into the determination of salary: difficulty of the job, level of experience, knowledge, competence and responsibility involved, and individual performance. The overall job market and prevailing rates of compensation by other employers are also considerations.

Top managers of smaller companies tend to deal with these factors as a matter of personal knowledge. Larger companies often turn to professional consultants for help. These consultants have one major advantage. Once they rate a given job by some numerical score, they can relate that to the compensation paid by all other companies in their large data base for all jobs with the same numerical score, on either a national or regional or industry basis. Further, from year to year, they can easily update the salary range that goes along with a given numerical rating.

Such a system has many advantages for larger companies, but not all executives will benefit from it. For example, when consultants first rate the executive jobs in a company and establish appropriate salary ranges for each, they almost invariably find some individuals who fall outside that range, with most deviations being above the upper limit. This usually is the result of seniority where the executive has received a raise each year, due to inflation, to the point that his salary has gone well above the appropriate job range.

For these rating systems to work properly, the basic facts must be communicated to each executive and they must know the salary range and median for their job. Thus the sad news for the executive above the upper limit is that no more raises will be forthcoming until inflation or competition raises the salary range for the job to the point that a further upward change can be justified. While this may be quite fair and equitable, it is not a very pleasant message for the supervisor to convey or for the executive to hear.

Nevertheless, there is much to be said for a general rating system of this type. While not perfect, it does translate what is necessarily a subjective judgment into a precise, numerical score that makes it possible to compare a job with all other jobs with a similar score. From the employer's viewpoint, of course, the goal should be to offer a fair and rewarding salary with due regard for competitive levels in the overall job market. If executives know they can leave the company and get a better salary elsewhere, they will certainly be tempted to make a change. Quite apart from the impact on morale, executive turnover can be very costly for any company.

There are also a number of fringe benefits that companies use to attract and keep good executives. Among these, stock options are a very popular choice. Their main attraction is that they place the executive in the same position as a stockholder in the company and provide the potential for significant capital gain if the company prospers and the stock price increases. Very often stock options are granted on the basis of individual or company performance, or both. The concept here is that the executive must do more than simply hold his job: Some specific performance is required as well to earn the right to a stock option.

Stock options may be vested over a period of time, such as 20 percent a year for five years. The same is true of various forms of deferred compensation and certain life insurance plans. A period of satisfactory service may be required for these benefits to accrue in full. The net result can be a rather powerful set of "golden handcuffs" that bind the executive to the company and thus help to minimize unwanted turnover.

There are a great variety of plans combining these and other benefits. If put together in such a way as to be fair to the company and its stockholders, any such plan that succeeds in achieving strong and proper motivation of executives can be highly beneficial to all concerned. Thus the subject of executive compensation merits, and usually receives, the careful attention of top managers and boards of directors.

SUMMARY

A good bonus system can be highly rewarding for the individual executive and for the company as well. It can do wonders to improve cooperation among all personnel throughout the company and help create an excellent state of general morale.

The best bonus system, in my experience, is one in which top executives share directly in the fortunes of the company, or a given subsidiary or division, come what may, good times and bad. In this fashion, the executive in effect becomes a partner in the company, and that is most likely to call forth the maximum in initiative and effort on behalf of the enterprise as a whole.

There are companies and situations in which such a system may not be feasible, and some other type of bonus plan must be installed, if any at all. But the closer this substitute can approach the partnership concept, the more likely it is to achieve the desired results for both the individual executive and the company.

In addition to salary and bonus, there are many other forms of executive compensation that, if properly designed in an overall plan, can be highly effective in terms of executive morale and performance. Executive compensation plans should receive thoughtful consideration in any well-managed company.

Equal consideration should also be given to salary and bonus incentives for other employees. Such incentives might include performance bonuses, pension plans, profit-sharing and thrift plans, and the like. Here again, making the employee a partner in the enterprise can add a great deal to both motivation and overall morale.

CHAPTER 23

THE ROLE OF THE CHIEF FINANCIAL OFFICER

HAVE YOU EVER wondered what the chief financial officer does for your company? Do you look upon this executive as some kind of glorified "bean counter"? If so, I would suggest that you modify that image. A more correct analogy is that of a physician charged with the responsibility of keeping the company in sound financial health, which can be a very difficult job indeed.

Typically, in addition to other duties, the chief financial officer, or CFO, is in charge of accounting for the company, and that in itself is no small task. Imagine the problems in keeping track of every asset and liability of the company and every transaction in the most minute detail in accordance with standard accounting principles. From these records, detailed monthly and annual reports must be prepared for management as well as the IRS and other government agencies. To add to the difficulty, there is always great pressure to complete all these reports in timely fashion.

At the end of the company's fiscal year, there is an audit by a firm of independent certified public accountants, which will then issue a report on whether the financial statements of the company fairly present its financial position. There are now eight big accounting firms in the country, called the "Big 8," which do most of this work for larger companies. Independent accountants are an unusual breed in that they do not work for the companies that retain them, but rather for the public at large, including stockholders, creditors, and others with a special interest in the financial status of the company.

In addition to this, most firms of any size now have an internal auditor, often with a considerable staff. This executive, as the name implies, is the company watchdog, checking practices and procedures in every department. If there is fraud anywhere in the company, which unfortunately does occur from time to time, some member of the internal auditing staff is likely to be the one who discovers it. No one is exempt from the scrutiny of this group, including the chief executive officer of the company. Most boards of directors now have an audit committee composed of outside directors, which meets regularly with the internal auditor on a confidential basis. Having a competent executive in this job, with an adequate staff, is the best possible insurance against improper practices anywhere in the company. Beyond this, much of the work of the internal auditing staff may be used by the independent firm of accountants, with a proportionate reduction in their fee for the annual audit.

If a company operates in various states and is subject to state and local taxes in each, a separate accounting department may be required to deal with nothing but these complexities. This, of course, is in addition to coping with the IRS. Contrary to popular opinion, most companies do pay a relatively huge income tax to the federal government. More is involved here than simply filing a tax return. Determination of what is and what is not a proper deductible expense item is often a matter of interpretation. For example, a company may consider a certain expenditure as a repair and maintenance item. As such, it would qualify for immediate tax deduction. But the IRS may take a contrary view, maintaining that it is a capital expenditure and hence must be amortized over a period of years. Large sums of money may be involved in questions of this kind and they must be resolved either by negotiation or by an appropriate appeal from the IRS decision.

PROVIDING NECESSARY CAPITAL

The CFO also has the major responsibility of seeing to it that the company always has the capital it needs to meet all of its various requirements and obligations. If the need is for long-term capital, he must turn to sources such as those described in Chapter 13. Expertise can be very valuable here because selecting the best source, and working out the optimum loan transaction, can save a company many millions of dollars over time.

In addition, the CFO must see to it that enough working capital is always on hand to meet the daily operating needs of the company, and must endeavor to do this in the most efficient way. The magnitude of that task becomes clear when it is realized that current assets make up about half the total assets of most companies and are quite difficult to control because of their volatility. Principal components of current assets are cash and negotiable securities, accounts receivable, and inventory. Each represents a separate problem. Let's first consider inventory. A CFO rarely has any direct control of inventory, but he must provide the necessary capital and therefore works closely with line executives who do control it.

Most service companies, of course, such as banks or insurance companies, are not dealing in merchandise and thus have no inventory problem. But manufacturers tend to be in a different position, with inventory in three stages: raw materials, work in process, and finished goods. Carrying inventory of this kind can cost a great deal of money. In addition to shipping, storage, and insurance charges, along with local property taxes, there is the cost of the capital required to maintain the inventory. Most companies will make a good deal of effort, therefore, to keep inventories down to a minimum working level.

Then, to complicate life, there may be a reverse problem in the inability to get raw materials and supplies when needed. If this happens to a manufacturing company, it can sometimes bring production to a halt. Inventory is an even more critical problem for retailers. Without the proper merchandise at the proper time, they must sustain a loss in sales and associated profit. The optimum inventory is hard to achieve and they can lose if it is too much and also if it is too little. All this is made even more difficult when sales are highly seasonal and the merchandise must be ordered many months before the actual sales period.

The CFO has more direct control over accounts receivable, another major component of current assets. Through the credit manager, he supervises the extension of credit, which is another balancing act: possible loss on a bad credit versus loss of sale if the credit is not extended. Once credit is granted, the emphasis shifts to collection of amounts due. This requires constant attention because typically the older an account, the greater the probability of loss.

Again, as in the case of inventory, capital is tied up in accounts receivable, and the CFO must see to it that the necessary capital is available. As companies grow, both inventories and accounts receivable will grow as well, and many small companies in particular have failed because this was not foreseen and the needed capital was simply not available.

To meet their daily operating needs, all companies need some liquid assets. Thus cash and marketable securities represent another main component of current assets, and here it is the job of the CFO to take maximum advantage of all the opportunities available. Most companies of any size now have some kind of formal cash management plan. Working with its lead bank, the company develops a program to obtain cash as quickly as possible and put it to productive use.

If the company operates in various states, for example, it may have set up a lockbox system in the key cities involved. Customers in a given area will send their check payments to a specific lockbox for collection by a local bank, which will wire the funds thus generated to the lead bank for credit to the company's account. In this way, no time is lost in making use of the funds available. If the company finds itself with excess cash on a given day, such funds can immediately be invested in some marketable security, perhaps overnight. Or if the company is short of cash, it may borrow from the bank to meet the temporary shortfall. Banks either charge an appropriate fee or require a proper compensating balance for these services.

On the other side of the ledger, the CFO must oversee the company's payment of its own bills. It is a waste of cash to pay bills before they are due, but it is usually desirable to take advantage of cash discounts for early payment. For example, an invoice received may specify payment in 30 days but grant a 2 percent discount if payment is made in 10 days. It may not sound like much, but note that failure to take this discount means that 2 percent is being given up for the privilege of keeping the money another 20 days. If you work this out, you will find that it represents an annual interest rate of about 43 percent, which is a very high price indeed for the use of money.

SUMMARY

The chief financial officer is a key executive in any company. He is not only responsible for accounting, in all of its intricate detail, but he must also see to it that the company has the capital it needs on both a permanent and temporary basis, on the best terms available.

He is also responsible, on a daily basis, for management and control of working capital. Current assets, in particular, not only represent a large share of the total assets of most companies, but also are highly volatile. Their proper control can add much to the overall efficiency of the company.

Important at all times, the job of the CFO becomes critical when a company is in financial trouble. In this situation, the competence of the CFO alone may spell the difference between ultimate survival and bankruptcy.

INDEX

Page numbers in *italics* refer to figures or tables.

ABOUT THE AUTHOR

Alan S. Donnahoe is currently Vice Chairman of Media General. During Media General's first nineteen years as a public company, he served as its chief executive officer, presiding over its growth from a small organization to a Fortune 500 company. He has also served on the boards of other major corporations. He lives in Richmond, Virginia.